Instructor's Manual *with* Tests

for

TEACHING CHILDREN TO READ AND WRITE

Instructor's Manual *with* Tests

for

TEACHING CHILDREN TO READ AND WRITE
Becoming an Influential Teacher

Robert B. Ruddell
University of California, Berkeley

Martha Rapp Ruddell
Sonoma State University, Rohnert Park

Allyn and Bacon
Boston · London · Toronto · Sydney · Tokyo · Singapore

ISBN 0-205-16510-9

Printed in the United States of America

10 9 8 7 6 5 4 3 2 1 00 99 98 97 96 95

TABLE OF CONTENTS

We wish to acknowledge Ms. Barbara Greybeck for her assistance in developing the short answer and multiple-choice questions for each chapter of <u>Teaching Children to Read and Write: Becoming an Influential Teacher</u>.

Instructor's Manual *with* Tests

for

TEACHING CHILDREN TO READ AND WRITE

A Special Note to the Instructor

Our Motivation for Writing this Text

We wrote <u>Teaching Children to Read and Write: Becoming an Influential Teacher</u> from our conviction and belief that teachers can and do make a difference in children's lives. When they do, these teachers are indeed influential teachers. Over our combined 60 years of teaching, both in the public schools and in the university, we have encountered many influential teachers. We have seen them teach and know the influence they have on children ranging from rescue of the struggling reader or writer, to special time and effort given to troubled or difficult children, to launching children into promising academic and life careers. We have also spent a significant part of our professional lives studying influential teachers, interviewing them, observing their teaching, and talking to students who identified them as influential in their lives. Our intent then, in writing this text is to share our observations and understandings of the philosophy, strategies, and instructional approaches used by influential teachers toward the goal of helping others to become influential teachers themselves.

As you will see in the Acknowledgement section of the book we each lived with an influential teacher from the time of our birth - our mothers. They, and other role models, shaped our own growth as teachers and guided our development over the years. It is our hope that <u>Teaching Children to Read and Write: Becoming and Influential Teacher</u> provides yet another form of guidance for developing teachers, whether they be student teachers working toward a credential or experienced teachers in an M.A. or doctoral program. We believe that <u>Teaching Children to Read and Write: Becoming an Influential Teacher</u> captures the very best of current theoretical knowledge and the very best of practical knowledge as well, with a bit of classroom wisdom thrown in for good measure. We hope you share our belief in the importance of the ideas in this text and that you will find success in using it in your classes.

Organization of the Text

The central focus of <u>Teaching Children to Read and Write: Becoming an Influential Teacher</u> is guiding the development of influential literacy teachers - teachers who understand language and literacy development, who know how to teach so that children's language and literacy growth are continually supported, and who are reflective and thoughtful about their own teaching and children's learning.

Chapters 1 through 11 present the basic concepts, approaches, and strategies essential for good literacy teaching. Topics range from the nature of early literacy acquisition and reading and writing processes to language and cultural diversity; from comprehension, vocabulary, and word analysis processes to literature and reader response; from evaluation of reading and writing progress to conferences with parents.

After developing these general concepts and strategies we then, in **Chapter 12**, put them into the classroom by examining three basic approaches to teaching reading and writing: the basal reader approach, the literature-based approach, and the whole language approach. It is our belief that every student should have some understanding of these three approaches that are used in the great majority of classrooms across the United States, Canada, and other English speaking countries. We begin Chapter 12 by examining basic philosophical tenets and beliefs for each approach and by providing examples of materials illustrating each. We make a distinction between literature-based and whole language approaches because of our conception of whole language instruction as fully integrated, project-based learning that is inquiry-driven and in which few, if any, boundaries exist between content areas. Literature-based instruction may be part of the whole language classroom, but in and of itself does not constitute full-blown whole language instruction.

In **Chapter 13** we explore classroom organization and management issues associated with implementation of each of these three approaches. And, because we believe early reading and writing are so important, we include a separate section addressing organization and management issues in kindergarten classrooms. Each section of this chapter examines underlying beliefs for a specific instructional approach (and early reading and writing development), develops options for the physical organization of the classroom and organization of the classroom day, and explores critical management issues ranging from managing project work, to scheduling reading groups, to routines and rules, to use of classroom volunteers and aides, to fostering children's independent work.

And finally, in **Chapter 14**, we urge both new and experienced teachers to continue their professional development and growth toward the influential teacher goal through contact with influential peer teachers and other school staff, participation in professional staff development opportunities, and membership and involvement in professional organizations. Our goal is to help teachers understand the continuous nature of change in schooling and the importance of adapting to change in becoming an influential literacy teacher.

More About the Book

In this book we urge each reader to become an influential teacher of reading and writing -- a teacher who will change children's lives. We believe each chapter provides a unique amalgam of theory and practice, and further that this amalgam is a necessary requisite for good teaching. It was fortuitous for us that this book was in progress during the time we completed editing Theoretical Models and Processes of Reading - Fourth Edition (Ruddell, Ruddell, & Singer, 1994). This effort involved an extensive and exhaustive review of the most recent literacy research to identify a multidisciplinary range of quality pieces to be included in that volume. As we worked we were resensitized to the critical need in our profession to "bridge build" between research and classroom practice. We believe we have accomplished this in Teaching Children to Read and Write: Becoming an Influential Teacher.

In developing what we hope your students will find a "friendly text" we speak as directly as possible to them and make every attempt to encourage them to interact with the text through the DOUBLE ENTRY JOURNAL, personal examples and illustrations, recall and analysis of their early reading and writing experiences, the HOW TO DO summaries, BUILDING TABLES and through the SUPPORTING ACTIVITIES. This INSTRUCTOR'S MANUAL is designed specifically for you and provides chapter summaries, teaching suggestions and evaluation options.

We fully believe that your use of this book builds a partnership that enables us to share responsibility with you for developing influential reading and writing teachers. We ask for your support in providing comments on features of the book that work well for you and for features that can be improved. We thus encourage you to correspond with us or to contact us in person at professional literacy conferences such as IRA, NCTE, NRC, or AERA. We sincerely hope that you will find the book challenging and interesting for your students and of value in your own teaching.

Key Features of the Book

A brief summary of the content and objectives for each chapter appears at the beginning of "Teaching Suggestions" for the chapter. This chapter overview, as well as each chapter summary, will prove to be of value in surveying (or reviewing) each chapter's contents. Other special features of the text, the benefit, use, and location of these features are described below.

DOUBLE ENTRY JOURNAL (DEJ).

Benefit: The DEJ is appears at the beginning and end of each chapter. This is an interactive strategy designed to stimulate students' thinking and draw on their prior knowledge about and previous experience with the general topic of the chapter to be read. The before-reading DEJ provides a focus on the chapter topic, activates prior knowledge, and, thus, guides students' reading of the text. The after-reading DEJ builds on the student's knowledge but combines it with the new ideas and strategies introduced in the chapter.

Use: To use the DEJ feature, ask your students get a notebook for recording their responses. The idea is to record responses before reading (the DEJ at the beginning of each chapter) on the LEFT-HAND page. Then after reading (the DEJ at the end of each chapter) to record DEJ responses on the RIGHT-HAND page facing the page where the before-reading response was recorded. In this way you can encourage your students to summon ideas knowledge they have on given topics before reading, extend and elaborate on these after reading, and make connections between the before- and after-reading ideas. A simple spiral notebook will do the job, although some students may prefer to integrate their DEJ responses with their class notes. The key point is to remind them to use the facing pages of the spiral notebook for their notes. We have found that encouraging students to share their notes with a class partner is valuable in producing reflective and integrative thinking, and we often open class by having students share DEJ insights in small groups..

Location: Beginning and end of each chapter.

HOW TO DO

Benefit: The HOW TO DO feature provides a summary of selected instructional strategies introduced in the book (Chapters 3, 4, 5, 6, 7, 9, and 10). Each HOW TO DO follows extended discussion of a specific instructional strategy and is intended to provide a no-nonsense, step-by-step list of things needed to plan, prepare and/or consider in order to use the strategy successfully in the classroom. Lesson plans can be easily developed from the HOW TO DO summaries. A major benefit of the HOW TO DO feature is that each is sufficiently explicit for text users to create lesson plans independently well after initial learning of the strategy occurs.

Use: After demonstration and/or discussion of the instructional strategy, walk student through the HOW TO DO steps. We frequently assign lesson plans (see Black Line Master 3-3) to give students practice applying strategies; we encourage students to use the HOW TO DO feature in developing their lesson plans.

Location: In Chapters 3, 4, 5, 6, 7, 9, and 10.

SUPPORTING ACTIVITIES

Benefit: The SUPPORTING ACTIVITIES are found at the end of each chapter and are intended to move the new concepts and strategies to application. Application will range from students recalling literacy experiences from their own schooling and introspection about and interpretation of these experiences to classroom observations of children and teachers to identify, describe, and interpret specific reading and writing experiences.

Use: We recommend that you identify and assign one or two supporting activities for each chapter; select those activities that you believe to be very important in acquiring key concepts for that chapter. Completion of these activities will reflect your students' understandings of and knowledge constructed for the chapter, and may represent an important part of your evaluation of student progress. It is also possible to have your students select one or two activities of their own choice as they build a portfolio reflecting their progress in your course. Selected SUPPORTING ACTIVITIES are expanded in the Teaching Suggestions section of this Instructor's Manual.

Location: End of all chapters.

BUILDING TABLES

Benefit: The BUILDING TABLES are found at the end of those chapters that introduce instructional strategies. The BUILDING TABLES explain to the student (1) the focus of each strategy used in a chapter, (2) how the strategy is best used (small groups, large groups), (3) how each strategy can be combined with strategies already developed in previous chapters, (4) preparation requirements (light, moderate, extensive), (5) additional resource needs, and (6) the page on which the HOW TO DO for that strategy appears.

The "May Be Combined With (known strategies)" section of the BUILDING TABLES is a key element intended to assist readers in making connections across chapters by showing how all of the instructional strategies may be usefully combined with other strategies. Beginning in Chapter Three, the "May Be Combined With (known strategies)" section builds from one chapter to the next. That is, the BUILDING TABLE for Chapter Three shows what strategies within that chapter may be usefully combined; the BUILDING TABLE for Chapter Four show combinations of strategies from Chapters Three and Four; the Chapter Five BUILDING TABLE includes strategies from Chapters Three, Four, and Five, and so on, so that by Chapter 10 all strategies in the text are incorporated into the "May Be Combined With (known strategies)" section.

Use: After walking through the HOW TO DO for each strategy turn to the BUILDING TABLE, note and discuss important planning features, and note possible combinations.

Location: End of Chapters 3, 4, 5, 6, 7, 9, and 10.

PHOTOS

Benefit: We selected photographs that we thought would add classroom reality and application to the text, as well as provide opportunity for an occasional smile of recognition or delight. Our intent in the selection process was to show teachers and children interacting in real classroom situations that demonstrate strategies, use small group discussions, and create authentic instructional situations.

Use: You may wish to comment on the photos or use them to stimulate partner or small group discussion.

Location: The 43 photos are placed strategically throughout the book. You will find 3 photos in each chapter except for Chapter 12 in which 4 photos are used.

INDEXES:

BENEFIT: We have developed two detailed indexes at the conclusion of the book to assist students in the location of key references and special topics. The first, the Author Index, identifies the author of every reference used in the text. Note that children's authors are identified in bold print. The second, the Subject Index, identifies key topics, instructional approaches, and instructional strategies, from "Achievement Diversity" to "Zone of Proximal Development."

Use: These two detailed indexes will be especially useful to students in easy and quick location of reference sources and discussions found in the text.

Location: End of text.

Instructor's Manual

This INSTRUCTOR'S MANUAL (IM) is designed specifically for you and provides two course syllabus prototypes: first, for a reading and writing methods course for student teachers; and second, for a first level reading and writing graduate course for students pursuing an M.A., Ed.D., or Ph.D. degree. The Instructor's Manual includes chapter summaries, teaching suggestions, and evaluation options. We have also developed Black Line Masters (BLM) to facilitate your teaching and the development of key concepts in each chapter.

COURSE SYLLABI

Benefit: We've included two prototype course syllabi in the Instructor's Manual to give you an idea of how we organize and teach this class. The first is for a class with student teachers and the second is for a class of experienced teachers. We thought you might find some good ideas for structuring your class.

<u>Use:</u> By all means creatively borrow our ideas in developing your course syllabus. We're rather certain that not everyone will choose to teach the class in the sequences we use; that's fine, but do note that we often make reference in later chapters to ideas presented earlier.

<u>Location:</u> Immediately following this discussion in the Instructor's Manual (beginning on page 11).

TEACHING SUGGESTIONS

<u>Benefit:</u> For each chapter of the text we provide a quick chapter summary and suggestions for teaching. Some of the teaching suggestions are expanded from the SUPPORTING ACTIVITIES list at the end of the chapter, others are taken from our own teaching repertoires. One or both of us have used and do use each activity. We identify the BLM selected for each chapter.

<u>Use:</u> Again, borrow, use, and adapt our suggestions as you will.

<u>Location:</u> Immediately following course syllabi.

STUDENT EVALUATION OPTIONS

<u>Benefit:</u> We're fully aware that Instructor philosophies regarding student evaluation vary widely from individual to individual. We have therefore provided a variety of student evaluation options ranging from observations of student class discussions and classroom application of ideas (see SUPPORTING ACTIVITIES) to short answer essay questions and multiple choice items. Student evaluation will also be based on the successful completion of various projects that you wish to include in your course ranging from lesson plans to term projects.

<u>Use:</u> The underlying belief we hold regarding student evaluation is that it should promote active thinking and classroom application of course concepts. You will find this perspective embodied in each of the SUPPORTING ACTIVITIES. We have also provided two options for use of the short answer essay and multiple choice test items. The first is using these items as a study guide for each chapter in such a way that students preview the items before reading the text and use the information from previewing to guide their reading. Note that we have provided page numbers to assist students in locating the chapter discussion that relates to each question. The second option is using these items as part of your overall evaluation of student progress. Our preference is using the two types of questions as a study guide to assist students in building concepts; we recommend that if you choose to use them as test items that you incorporate other assessment strategies as well (projects, portfolios, etc.).

In the Sample Course Syllabus for Student Teachers beginning on page 11 of this Instructor's Manual you will find how one of us has chosen to use portfolio assessment in her courses. Portfolio assessment in this rendition has seven major components:

1. <u>Providing the portfolio for the students</u>. The ones with side pockets and a three-hole binder with brads work just fine. These are rather cheaply available at discount office supply stores.

2. <u>Awarding grades for the portfolio at both midterm and end-of-semester</u>. In my first portfolio assessment iteration I didn't award grades at midterm because I wanted to keep risk down; what I did do was provide lots of written feedback. The students didn't like that - they felt their whole grade depended on the end-of-semester evaluation. I rearranged my objectives so that the first four objectives correspond to the first half of my class; students fulfill those objectives for their midterm grade. I allow anyone who makes a grade lower than C- to resubmit her or his midterm portfolio.

3. <u>Stating explicitly what students are expected to demonstrate</u>. Since I give very wide leeway for students to select the portfolio artifacts I want to make sure that they know what I expect of them. My biggest task is getting students to synthesize their learning in their rationale statements. I spend lots of time in class discussing the importance of this. I also emphasize repeatedly that I don't want portfolios filled with unexplained materials, nor do I want students simply to hand back the handouts I gave them. <u>Everything</u> is to be connected to an objective. I also remind students often that this particular portfolio is for the purpose of demonstrating what they've learned in this class - everything must be connected to this course content. I ask them to keep that overall objective firmly in mind

4. <u>Providing explicit and complete grading criteria</u>. The grading rubric you see in the course syllabus is one of my newest additions to portfolio grading. I developed the rubric **with a class of students** and will modify and revise it each semester in each class so that we have an agreed-upon understanding of what separates the wheat from the chaff portfolio-wise. This not only helps students clarify their thinking as they assemble their portfolios, but helps me clarify my thinking while grading. I keep the rubric in front of me alongside the list of what students are to show for each criterion as I grade.

5. <u>Reporting fully and richly to students about their portfolios</u>. Portfolios are a lot of work, and I feel strongly that students deserve more that cryptic comments and margin notes for the work they do. I don't **ever** write in the portfolios; I've set up a macro on my wordprocessing system that lists the objective criteria (i.e., what students are to "show" for each objective) on the left side of the page and the rubric (Exceptional, Thorough, Adequate, Inadequate) across the top. I wordprocess an <u>X</u> for each criterion and then

write a narrative response for each objective and one for the portfolio overall. These tend to be very personalized and personal. I return a copy with the portfolio and keep one for my records.

6. <u>Giving students time to share their portfolios</u>. At midterm we do a quick-share - a half-hour or so when students at their small group tables show their portfolios to one another. I sometimes have them do this in partners. At the end of the semester we use the scheduled date of the final (since I give no final) for students to do a more formal sharing of their portfolio with a small group. I ask them each sharing time to talk about what they learned as they assembled their portfolios. Students like this; they are proud of their work and want the reinforcement that showing it to others brings.

7. <u>Understanding that portfolio assessment is organic</u>. One of the first lessons I learned about portfolio assessment is that it's constantly changing. I've yet to do portfolios exactly the same way in any two consecutive semesters. You learn from it every time you use it; and now that so many colleagues are using one form or another of portfolio assessment, you keep getting new, wonderful ideas (I spend an awful lot of time at professional conferences these days trading portfolio assessment ideas with friends and folks). Here are my two latest modifications (they're not fully worked out yet but soon will be): a) I'm going to remove/modify/combine one or more objectives to make room for my students to formulate their <u>own</u> objective for this class and meet it (thank you, MaryEllen Vogt); and b) I'm going to establish portfolio working groups or partnerships for students to support each other in developing their portfolios (thank you, P. David Pearson) - I've always encouraged collaboration; now I'm going to help get it started.

We encourage you to try some form of portfolio assessment. If you feel strongly about giving exams, make them part of the portfolio and make them flexible so students can reveal their thinking behind any a, b, c choices they make.

<u>Location:</u> The SUPPORTING ACTIVITIES are found at the end of each chapter. The short answer and multiple choice items are placed at the conclusion of Teaching Suggestions for each chapter in this Instructor's Manual.

BLACK LINE MASTERS (BLM)

<u>Benefit:</u> We have included a set of BLACK LINE MASTERS from selected pages of the text and from handouts we have developed for our students. Each BLACK LINE MASTER is keyed to the specific chapter for its intended use (e.g., BLM 1-1, BLM 1-2, etc.).

<u>Use:</u> Each BLM may be used to make an overhead transparency to

accompany your class discussions or photocopied for a handout (reproduction permission is granted). Suggestions for use of each BLM are noted in the "Teaching Suggestions" for the appropriate chapter.

<u>Location:</u> The BLACK LINE MASTERS are found at the end of this Instructor's Manual.

Notes:

EDUC 462
Language and Literacy in Elementary Schools

Martha Rapp Ruddell
Office: STV 3096C
Phone: (sch) 707-664-2556; (hm) 510-339-0701
Fax: 510-339-9414
e-mail: martha.ruddell@sonoma.edu

Office Hours:
M 2:30-3:30 p.m.
T 2:00-4:00 p.m..
Th 11:00 a.m.-12:00 noon by appt. only

<u>Course Text:</u>

Ruddell, R. B., & Ruddell, M. R. (1995). <u>Teaching Children to Read and Write:</u>
   <u>Becoming an Influential Teacher</u>. Boston: Allyn & Bacon.

Handouts - $3.00 fee

<u>Course Objectives:</u>

To develop

1. <u>Knowledge of the theories and principles of children's language and literacy</u>
    <u>development from emergent and early reading and writing through</u>
    <u>conventional, accomplished reading and writing</u>. The focus here is on your
    becoming a teacher who is an **informed decision-maker**, one who
    understands children's language and literacy development and who makes
    instructional decisions based on that understanding. You will begin the
    never-ending process of articulating your own theories of language and
    literacy learning.

2. <u>Knowledge of current approaches - basal reader, literature-based, and whole</u>
    <u>language - for teaching reading and writing</u>. You need to know what's "out
    there," what constitutes the most commonly used literacy instructional
    approaches in schools, the theory that underlies each, and the means for
    implementing each. Then you'll need to begin making some decisions
    about your affinity for each and how you will teach reading and writing
    from emergent and early literacy development through accomplished
    reading and writing.

3. <u>Skill in using reading and writing instructional strategies</u>. You will learn
    how to use numerous means for engaging student attention, guiding
    children's reading and writing, and assisting children in becoming strategic
    readers, writers and learners. You will further learn how to situate various
    instructional strategies into your own theory base and into your choice of
    instructional approach.

11

4. <u>Understanding of the history of literacy instruction in the U.S. and the relationship between that history and your own literacy development</u>. It is important, I think, that you know about the past and have glimpses of the future in order to understand what it is we are doing today. By looking at your own literacy development from both an individual and historical perspective, you begin to understand the complexity of forces that impact the education of individual students.

5. <u>Awareness of diversity in student abilities, cultural backgrounds and language, and ability to use these understandings to develop appropriate instructional practices</u>. We live in diverse world and we daily teach students whose culture, primary language and reality are different from our own. We must - all of us - prepare ourselves to meet these students' needs so that they become accomplished learners in our classrooms. Language and literacy development are critical aspects of this process. We will spend a great deal of time throughout the semester addressing issues of first and second language development, bilingualism, language use transitions, and second language pedagogy.

6. <u>Skill in developing students' subject area literacy abilities</u>. Learning requires students to become accomplished language users and readers and writers in subject areas, and to develop and extend their language and literacy abilities continually. To do that, students must read and write in every subject area, interact with their peers, and develop understandings that go across subject discipline boundaries. Here, again, we will address learning issues for students whose first language is not English and learn how to develop Specially Designed Academic Instruction (SDAI) through sheltered English lessons and other means.

7. <u>Knowledge of authentic reading and writing assessment techniques and skill in using them; understanding of formal testing instruments; ability to evaluate instructional materials</u>. You will need to be able to evaluate informally, and on a daily and minute-to-minute basis, how children's language and literacy are progressing. You will learn how to do this, and just as important, how to record and document your findings. You will also be expected to understand and interpret to students and their parents the results of school-, district- and state-wide testing programs, and to evaluate textbooks and other instructional materials.

8. <u>Knowledge of interesting trade books for children to read, including books written by, for and about people of a culture different from your own</u>. It all comes down to cliches: "There's more to life than learning." "All work and no play makes Jack/Jill a dull boy/girl." "Knowing how to read and choosing not to is infinitely worse than not knowing how to read." Take your pick or use all three. You need to do more than just teach; you need to teach, and "reach," KIDS. This one's for them.

Course Requirements:

1. **Attendance and participation in class.** This is a "hands on" course in which many instructional techniques are demonstrated in class and much of the learning takes place in small and large group discussion. You will find it almost impossible to recreate class events by borrowing someone else's notes. Plan to attend all classes <u>for the full time period</u>. If you are unable to attend a class meeting, please notify me in advance.

2. **Completion of assigned and outside readings and activities.** Built into the text are <u>D</u>ouble <u>E</u>ntry <u>J</u>ournal activities (DEJs) that you will complete each week. You will need a separate notebook (spiral bound or otherwise) specifically designated as your Double Entry Journal. <u>You will spend a significant amount of time each week working from your DEJ entries; be SURE you have completed them and are prepared to participate in class.</u>

3. **Completion of lesson plans as assigned.** You will write lesson plans for the types of teaching and learning we experience and discuss in class. I will give you plenty of information and assistance in writing the lesson plans; however, you may feel a little frustrated at first. Don't worry. You'll get better quickly.

4. **Compilation of an annotated bibliography of good books for children to read with emphasis on books for, by, and about people of a culture different from your own.** The goal here is for you to become knowledgeable about books that the <u>students you will be teaching</u> like to read. Include a minimum of 15 book titles - 5 great books you remember from your own childhood, and <u>10 (or more) books you've never read before in your life</u>. Find books that reflect positively on diversity in our society; find new, exciting, "with it" books that will interest today's and tomorrow's children; read about people and cultures you know very little about. Balance your selection of "classics" with plenty of recent titles.

    This bibliography is intended to be something you **actually use when you teach school**; something that grows right along with you and your years of teaching. Handwrite your annotations on file cards (whatever size you like) or use your computer. <u>Choose your top five titles, type them with the annotations on a single page, and make enough copies to distribute to each class member and me.</u> See the last page of the course syllabus for the bibliographic form and sample annotations.

5. **Compilation of a Performance Portfolio.**

Course Grading:

Your grade in this class will be based primarily on the work you submit in your

PERFORMANCE PORTFOLIO. The purpose for the portfolio this semester is for you to demonstrate your learning in this class; later, it may be the foundation for development of a professional portfolio that you maintain throughout your teaching career.

Your performance portfolio will be submitted for two (2) evaluations: midterm and end-of-semester. You will earn a portfolio grade for each evaluation that will then be used to compute your final grade; this will be done by determining the arithmetical average of your midterm and final portfolio evaluations.

Attendance, class participation and adherence to assigned due dates will be considered in the assignment of a final grade for the course.

Midterm and End-of-Semester Portfolio Evaluation

At midterm, **March 21**, your portfolio will be submitted for evaluation of your performance on the first four (4) course objectives detailed on the first two pages of this course syllabus.

Your second portfolio evaluation will occur at the end of the semester. On **May 16** you will submit your final portfolio demonstrating knowledge, understanding and ability for objectives five through eight (5-8) for the course. Your annotated bibliography will constitute full completion of requirements for Objective #8.

Portfolio Contents

For each portfolio evaluation (midterm and end-of-semester), you are to provide evidence of any type you wish to demonstrate that you have achieved the course objectives for that evaluation. To do this you are to

1.   Gather, collect and organize your artifacts for each objective. Artifacts may be completed (or extended) DEJs, lesson plans, notes from class, notes and other information from other classes, notes or other information from classroom observations, and/or any combination of the above or other materials. Artifacts do not have to be from this class, but they must be related to this class. Organize the materials you are submitting in your portfolio, making sure to label everything clearly so I will know what you're submitting for each objective.

2.   For each objective write a rationale statement to demonstrate your knowledge and abilities with respect to the objective. Specify

   a.   What artifact(s) you chose to submit

   b.   Why you chose it/them

14

c.   How your artifacts link to the objective itself.

REMEMBER: THE POINT OF PRESENTING ARTIFACTS AND ACCOMPANYING RATIONALE STATEMENTS IS TO DEMONSTRATE YOUR LEARNING IN THIS COURSE.

Be sure to provide a rationale statement for ALL DESIGNATED OBJECTIVES.

Your rationale statements are the synthesis points of your portfolio; be sure they are fully and completely done. They should represent your very best work. Your rationale statements must be typed.

3.   Be sure to show explicitly how materials from other classes/experiences relate specifically to the content and substance of this course. Do not submit unexplained printed matter or notes.

Grading Criteria

I will evaluate your portfolio and the work you submit according to the following:

1.   How fully and completely you demonstrate knowledge, understanding and application of each objective. I will look for both breadth and depth in your artifacts and your rationale statements.

2.   The quality of your written rationale statements. Do not confuse quality with bulk; more is not necessarily better. However, DO develop your rationale statements sufficiently to demonstrate your knowledge and ability for each objective. If you can do that in a few elegant words, so much the better.

3.   The quality of your lesson plans. Lesson planning is the appropriate application of many concepts and objectives of this course.

4.   I will rate your submitted materials using the following rubric:

Exceptional:
        Information is thoughtfully synthesized
        Information goes well beyond the required
        Information is presented imaginatively and creatively
        Artifacts demonstrate deep understanding
        Artifacts are rich, in-depth, original
        Rationale is explicit, clearly stated, and full
        Rationale shows clear linkages of artifacts to objectives

Thorough:
        Information is well thought out and organized
        Information is clearly presented

15

Artifacts demonstrate clear understanding
Rationale is clear, specific, and varied
Rationale shows linkages of artifacts to objectives

Adequate:
Information is minimal and accurate
Artifacts demonstrate understanding
Rationale show some linkages of artifacts to objectives
Every criterion is addressed

Inadequate:
Information is missing, inaccurate, and/or muddled
Artifacts are incomplete and/or lacking in breadth and depth
Rationale shows no or little linkage of artifacts to objectives
Every criterion is not addressed

The following specific criteria should guide your portfolio development for each objective:

Objectives One and Two -

Show that you understand how children become literate.

Show that you understand the key characteristics of basal reader, literature-based, and whole language instruction.

Show how you plan to approach reading and writing instruction in your classroom.

Objective Three -

Show that you can use and/or adapt a variety of instructional strategies that are congruent with the literacy instructional approach you have chosen.

Objective Four -

Show that you have reflected on your own literacy development.

Show linkages between your literacy development and the history of U.S. literacy instruction.

Objective Five -

Show that you understand how cultural, language, academic and other differences may affect students' learning in your classroom.

Show that you can use and/or adapt instructional strategies that 1) guide students' reading and writing, and 2) accommodate for cultural, language, academic, and other differences.

Objective Six -

Show that you can use and/or adapt instructional strategies for guiding students' reading and writing across the curriculum. Be sure to include cooperative/collaborative and SDAI learning in your lesson and unit planning.

Objective Seven -

Show how you can use authentic, informal assessments to evaluate students' reading and writing.

Show that you understand appropriate uses and interpretations of formal assessment instruments

Show your ability to evaluate instructional materials using a variety of evaluative approaches and instruments.

Objective Eight -

Annotated Bibliography.

NOTE: If you satisfy these requirements minimally, you can expect an average grade (C). Superior grades (A and B) are achieved by evidence of superior accomplishment.

Course Outline

DATE	TOPIC	ASSIGNMENT
Jan 24	Introduction and Course Description	
Jan 31	Becoming an Influential Teacher Reading and Writing Processes	Chapter 1 Chapter 2 DEJ Chapter 2
Feb 7	Emergent and Early Reading and Writing	Chapter 3 DEJ

DATE	TOPIC	ASSIGNMENT
Feb 14	Approaches for Literacy Instruction	Chapter 12 DEJ
Feb 21	Organizing and Guiding Literacy Instruction Lesson Planning	Chapter 13 DEJ
Feb 28	Comprehension Instruction	Chapter 4 DEJ
Mar 7	Vocabulary and Comprehension Connections	Chapter 5 DEJ
Mar 14	Literature Response	Chapter 6 DEJ
Mar 21	Portfolio Sharing The Writing Workshop	Chapter 7 **PORTFOLIOS DUE**
Mar 28	Reading and Writing Across the Curriculum	Chapter 9 DEJ
Apr 4	Diversity in the Classroom	Chapter 10 DEJ
Apr 11	Word Analysis	Chapter 8 DEJ
Apr 18	SPRING BREAK - NO CLASS	
Apr 25	Authentic Assessment in Classrooms Continuing Professional Development	Chapter 11 DEJ Chapter 14
May 2	Portfolio Preparation	
May 9	Bibliography Sharing and Reading to Peers	Bibliography Handout Due
May 16	FINAL CLASS - 5:00-6:50 Portfolio Sharing	**PORTFOLIOS DUE**

Annotated Bibliography Samples

Please follow the bibliographic style shown below for each book title:

Ringgold, Faith (1991). Tar Beach. New York: Crown Books. ISBN 0-517-58030-6

Cassie Louise Lightfoot lives in Harlem in 1939. She and her family picnic and play on the roof of their building - Tar Beach. Cassie feels the "stars come down around her" on Tar Beach and from this feeling flies in her imagination around the city righting wrongs and making life better for her and her family.

Originally part of Ringgold's story quilt (currently hanging at the Guggenheim), Tar Beach is illustrated with Ringgold's acrylic on canvas paintings; each is bordered by quilt patterns taken from the original story quilt. This is a gorgeous book in every way: The story is both magical and autobiographical, illustrations are beautiful, and the reproduction of the original story quilt at the end of the story, along with an extended biography of Ringgold, gives one a sense of completion.

Read to all ages
Grades 3 - up

_____

Martin, Bill Jr., Illus., Eric Carle (1967). Brown Bear, Brown Bear, What Do You See? New York: Henry Holt and Company. ISBN 0-8050-0201-4

"Brown Bear, Brown Bear, what do you see?" "I see a redbird looking at me." "Redbird, redbird, what do you see?" "I see a yellow duck looking at me." So opens Bill Martin Jr.'s classic, predictable book. The delightful chants continue through the book with Eric Carle's equally delightful illustrations adding to the fun. The very youngest children quickly perceive the pattern and join the chant. This text then becomes an easy pattern for children to emulate in their own story writing.

Grades K-2

_____

Kane, Herb Kawainui (1987). <u>Pele Goddess of Hawaii's Volcanoes</u> (2nd ed.). Captain Cook, HI: The Kawainui Press.

Written and illustrated by artist Herb Kane (KAH-nay), this book tells of the goddess Pele and of ancient Hawai'i. The text is lyrical - "She is Pele-honua-mea, Pele of the sacred land. She is Pele-´ai-honua, Pele the eater of land, when she devours the land with her flames" - and many of the illustrations are beautifully reproduced art. The myths, legends, traditions, and folklore of Hawai'i are faithfully retold here signaled by the traditionally correct spellings of Hawai'ian words (e.g., "Hawai'i" rather than "Hawaii"). Kane presents the old culture in his own modern day voice, uses and defines many Hawai'ian words, and interweaves myth with his own experience. A sumptuous work of nonfiction and a wonderful addition to any class library.
Grades 4-8

Paterson, Katherine (1980). <u>Jacob Have I Loved</u>. New York: Avon Books (Paperback). ISBN 0-380-56499-8.

Louise and Caroline are twins growing up on a Chesapeake Bay island where their father's family has lived for over 200 years. Louise lives in the shadow of Caroline - the bright, beautiful, popular younger twin. Taunted by her bitter grandmother, "Jacob have I loved, but Esau have I hated. . .", Louise feels unhappy, slighted, and robbed of everything that could be good in her life. Louise rejects the typical teen girl activities and turns her attention to learning the ways of watermen on the island. Finally as an adult she leaves the island and finds peace.

One of Katherine Paterson's many beautiful books (<u>Bridge to Terabithia</u>, <u>The Great Gilly Hopkins</u>). This one explores the difficult issues surrounding sibling rivalry and the disruptions caused by family members' anger and long-lasting bitterness. As usual, Paterson addresses delicate issues, and, as usual, she does it with tenderness and class. This book will undoubtedly appeal more to girls than to boys, but the themes addressed go beyond gender.

Grades 5-8

Sample Course Syllabus for First Level Graduate Course
(M.A., Ed.D., Ph.D Students)

ELL 242A - Trends and Issues in Reading and Literacy Instruction

Robert B. Ruddell
Phone: 510-642-0746 (Office)
        510-339-8272 (Home)
Fax: 510-339-9414
e-mail: rruddell@uclink2.berkeley.edu

Office Hours:
Monday, 1:00-4:00
Wednesday, 1:00-4:00
Class Meeting, Monday, 4:00-7:00

<u>Course Text:</u>

Ruddell, R.B. & Ruddell, M.R. (1995). <u>Teaching Children to Read and Write:</u>
    <u>Becoming an Influential Teacher</u> Boston, MA: Allyn and Bacon.

Reserved Readings in Library

Selected Handouts

<u>Course Objectives:</u>

ELL 242A, Trends and Issues in Reading Instruction, is designed to:

1.   Increase your understanding of reading and literacy development of the beginning and skilled reader;

2.   Examine the most recent thinking about the nature of reading and language development;

3.   Introduce you to classroom-based instructional strategies and approaches designed to increase your teaching effectiveness. We will study the interrelated nature of reading and writing processes and the development of optimal instructional conditions for reading instruction in a language rich environment. Criteria for the evaluation of teaching and curriculum materials will be a natural outcome of our discussion.

4.   Provide opportunity to develop an individual term project consistent with your professional goals and objectives. The following topic areas suggest the range of individual projects that may be pursued:

    1)   Formulation of a rationale and curriculum organization plan for one aspect of a language based reading and/or writing program, e.g., literature-based, integrated reading and writing program, word analysis program for whole language.

    2)   Evaluation of the reading and/or writing program you may be

21

currently using in your classroom, or school district, with recommendations for improving the effectiveness of instruction.

3) Formal evaluation of the reading and/or writing program used in your school or school district with recommendations for improvement.

4) Development of a reading and/or writing integrated unit and field testing the unit in your classroom or in a selected classroom, e.g., comprehension or literature areas.

5) Development of a detailed course syllabus for teaching a future reading/language course to pre-service or in-service teachers (including sample materials to be used).

6) Completion of a detailed literature review in a selected area of reading and literacy development.

7) Design and completion of a short term action research project on a selected area of reading and/or writing instruction, including rationale, design, discussion of your observations and implications for practice. Such projects may range from the exploration of reader response groups and writing workshop to the study of content area writing and sheltered English.

8) Other - to be determined on by individual student goals.

Your proposed project should be formulated early in the semester and approved in our joint discussion before proceeding with the project. Should you be an Ed.D or Ph.D student you should consider the potential the project may have for your future inservice work or for teaching in higher education.

Procedures:

The following procedures will be followed in the course development:

1. Specific readings will be developed through discussion and classroom demonstrations.

2. Course topics will pursued through small group interaction.

3. Emphasis will be placed on theoretical aspects of reading and writing teaching and the identification of curriculum implications and practices.

4. Individual student projects will be shared with the class toward the end of the semester.

5. The term project will be due on the last day of class.

<u>Participation:</u>

Course participation is expected in lecture and small group settings. Specifically the following areas are important:

1. Class reading assignments will be identified at least one week before discussion. These should be carefully read and you should be prepared to offer your analysis and insights regarding the readings. You will find the use of the Double Entry Journal (DEJ) helpful in focusing and integrating your reading (see p. xi of the Preface in the text).

2. Class participation is valued and will be based on the readings and applied course experiences.

3. Attendance in class is very important. Should a personal emergency arise it is important that you let me know this as soon as possible. This will assist me in the design of small group team projects. Please call our Education in Language and Literacy Secretary, at <u>642-0746</u>, or my office, at <u>642-3988</u>, to inform me or to leave a message.

4. Completion of your individual term project will be <u>due on the last day of class.</u> Here are several suggestions which I ask that you follow in completing your paper:

    1) <u>Be sure to place a table of contents at the front of your paper.</u> This will assist you final revisions and assist me in obtaining an overview of your paper. Also, be sure to number the pages in your paper.

    2) Use the <u>Publication Manual of the American Psychological Association</u> (Third Edition, 1983) for references and formatting of your paper. This reference system is used throughout the Ruddell and Ruddell text being used in this class. However, should you wish to purchase a copy of the APA Manual a copy can be obtained at ASUC Bookstore.

    3) Make sure that your paper follows a logical organization with the following features:
        -- Clear introductory statement indicating need, purpose, intent, and expectations in the development of your paper.
        -- A brief discussion indicating how your paper will unfold and develop.
        -- Development of your discussion guided by your purpose, intent, and logic.
        -- Conclusions which are clearly drawn from you discussion. Implications for practice and possible research should also be developed.
        -- Complete bibliography following the APA format.

4)   You will be asked to make a brief 5 to 10 minute presentation of your project to the class at the end of the semester. A one or two page abstract of your project with a selected bibliography (5 to 10 items using the APA format) should be prepared for each member of the class. This abstract must be ready for distribution during the class period <u>preceding</u> your presentation.

5)   I will schedule a meeting with you early in the semester to discuss your term project. In preparation for this meeting I ask that you provide a two page discussion, which includes the following:

   (1)   A one paragraph statement of the problem. In short, what is the key question(s) or problem(s) you are pursuing? what is it that you want to accomplish in your project?

   (2)   A paragraph stating why this is an important area for you to pursue.

   (3)   One page that briefly describes the rationale for your project. This is simply a brief discussion of the logic which underlies your proposed project. The discussion should include references to indicate who and what kind of reading you have been doing in your area of interest.

   (4)   A time line for the rest of the semester, by week, specifying your plan of action in completing the project by the end of the semester.

Evaluation:

1.   Attendance is of critical importance in order for you to participate actively in the discussions.

2.   Preparation for class as reflected in you participation and discussion of the readings, small group projects, and individual written assignments is essential.

3.   The completion of your individual paper is an important part of the final grade. Remember the final date for submitting the paper is the last day of class.

4.   The final exam will provide opportunity to synthesize the major areas of our discussion.

5.   The final grade will be based on class participation (25%), the final exam (25%) and your term project (50%).

Course Outline

DATE	TOPIC

Aug 22   <u>Introduction and Course Description</u>

Aug 29   <u>Becoming an Influential Reading and Writing Teacher - Chapter 1;</u>
<u>Coming to Know the Reading and Writing Processes: Understanding</u>
<u>Meaning Making - Chapter 2 (Initiate)</u>

Sept 5   Labor Day - No Class

Sept 12   <u>Coming to Know the Reading and Writing Processes- Chapter 2</u>
<u>(Complete); Understanding the Beginning Steps: Early Reading and</u>
<u>Writing Development - Chapter 3</u>

Sept 19   <u>Developing Reading Comprehension: Using Instructional Strategies to</u>
<u>Develop Higher Level Thinking - Chapter 4</u>

Sept 26   <u>Building Vocabulary and Comprehension Connections - Chapter 5</u>

Oct 3   <u>Using Literature and Reader Response to Enhance Attitudes and</u>
<u>Comprehension - Chapter 6</u>

Oct 10   <u>Using Word Analysis Strategies to Develop Reader Independence:</u>
<u>Transforming Print to Meaning - Chapter 8</u>

Oct 17   <u>Guiding Children's Writing - Chapter 7</u>

Oct 24   <u>Developing Children's Literacy Abilities in Content Areas - Chapter 9</u>

Oct 31   <u>Understanding Language, Cultural, and Achievement Diversity in the</u>
<u>Classroom - Chapter 10; Evaluating Children's Progress in Reading</u>
<u>and Writing - Chapter 11 (Initiate)</u>

Nov 7   <u>Evaluating Children's Progress in Reading and Writing - Chapter 11</u>
<u>(Complete); Examining Instructional Approaches: Basal Reader,</u>
<u>Literature-Based, Whole Language, and Supplementary Programs -</u>
<u>Chapter 12 (Initiate)</u>

Nov 14   <u>Examining Instructional Approaches - Chapter 12 (Complete);</u>
<u>Organizing and Managing Classrooms for Literacy Learning - Chapter</u>
<u>13 (Initiate)</u> (Take Home Final Exam Distributed)

DATE   TOPIC

Nov 21   <u>Organizing and Managing Classrooms for Literacy Learning -</u>
                <u>Chapter 13 (complete); Continuing Professional Change</u>
                <u>and Growth: Reading the Influential Teacher Goal -</u>
                <u>Chapter 14</u>

Nov 28   Individual Reports; Final Exam and Term Paper Due

TEACHING SUGGESTIONS BY CHAPTER

The following suggestions are designed to support your use of this textbook in your course. Suggestions for each chapter are presented in three categories. The first, Chapter Summary, provides a brief overview of the chapter and identifies key chapter objectives. The second, Teaching Suggestions, develops a series of teaching ideas that we have used that have proven to be highly effective in promoting student interaction, application of ideas, and active thinking. You will find that some of these Suggestions are parallel to the Supporting Activities found at the end of each chapter. And third, Evaluation Options, suggests a variety of approaches to the evaluation of student progress. We have left space at the end of each chapter set of Teaching Suggestions for your own notes as you use <u>Teaching Children to Read and Write: Becoming an Influential Teacher</u> in your course.

<u>Notes:</u>

Chapter 1. Becoming an Influential Reading and Writing Teacher

Chapter Summary

This chapter is designed to establish the three goals of the text. These are:
1) To increase your students' understanding of children's reading and writing development; 2) To extend their understanding in a meaningful way by examining the most recent theories and research about the nature of reading and writing; and 3)) To introduce classroom based instructional strategies and approaches that will help your students become highly effective teachers of reading and writing, and influential ones as well.

The chapter also develops a challenge for your students - that of becoming an influential teacher who will have a major influence on the personal and academic success of their students. Shared beliefs of influential teachers are discussed and students are encouraged to reflect on their own former influential teachers and identify similar and different characteristics. A brief discussion of teaching expectations and a "snapshot" of reading instruction across the nation is developed.

The chapter concludes with a "Preview of Chapters Ahead" and reiterates the challenge to become an Influential Teacher

Teaching Suggestions

1. Use the Double Entry Journal (DEJ), eliciting memories of early reading and writing experiences and influential teachers, in small and large group discussions (see page xi of the text and the earlier discussion in this Instructor's Manual for ideas on using the DOUBLE ENTRY JOURNAL).

2. Encourage your students to recall their earliest memories of reading full length or "chapter" books. In small groups ask them to identify one or more of their earliest chapter books and recall their emotional response to this literature. Key ideas from the small groups may then be shared with the total class followed by your synthesis and summary.

3. Encourage your students to return to their memories of their Influential Teacher(s) (see Table 1-1, page 8 of text). In small group discussions ask your students to consider ways in which this teacher(s) may have influenced their personal beliefs about teaching effectiveness. Make an overhead transparency of Table 1-1 (BLM 1-1 - See Black Line Masters at the end of this Instructor's Manual) and provide a brief overview of the "Shared Beliefs of Influential Teachers About Teaching" (also Table 1-2, p. 10 in the text). Encourage your students to consider how their beliefs are similar to and different from those of the Influential Teachers.

4. Have your students complete the Personal Belief System checklist found on

page 23 of the text and indicate their level of agreement or disagreement. (You may wish to photocopy this checklist from BLM 1-2 for student response). Use partner teams for students to compare their responses by exploring reasons for agreement or disagreement on each item. You may elect to identify two or three items, e.g., Items 2,7,9, for total class discussion.

Black Line Masters (BLM) for Chapter 1

BLM 1-1 (text p. 10) Shared Beliefs of Influential Teachers About Teaching
BLM 1-2 (text p. 23) Identifying My Personal Belief System: Teaching
Reading and Writing Skills

Evaluation Options

1.   Your observations of student participation in small and large group discussions.

2.   Your evaluation of student responses to Short Answer Essay Questions (see items below). Please note that we have provided page numbers that are keyed to the text indicating where the content related to each question is located. You may wish to use these questions as a study guide for you students rather than as an evaluation option.

3.   Your evaluation of Multiple Choice Questions (see items below). Again, you will find each question is keyed to the text content and you may wish to use these questions as a study guide.

4.   Your evaluation of students' portfolios.

<u>Short Answer Essay Questions</u>

1. Identify one of your own influential teachers and discuss what characteristics made him/her effective. Compare these characteristics with the list generated by Ruddell and his colleagues in Table 1-2. (p. 10)

2. Which of the characteristics of influential teachers in Table 1-2 do you feel are most important for elementary school teachers and why? (p. 10)

3. Currently, what do you feel are the most pressing issues in literacy in this country?(pp. 11-13)

4. Why is it important to understand the relationship between theory and practice in literacy instruction?(pp. 6-7)

Multiple Choice Questions

1. In studies of influential teachers by Ruddell and Haggard (1982) and Ruddell and Kern (1986): (p. 9)
    a. high and low achievers perceived their teachers in much the same way
    b. high achievers believed that quality of instruction was most important
    c. low achievers believed that an understanding of learner potential was the most important characteristic for effective teaching
    d. none of the above

2. According to studies by Ruddell and his colleagues, which of the following are characteristics of influential teachers? (pp. 8-10)
    a. they stimulate intellectual curiosity by tapping into students' internal motivation
    b. they use a whole language approach in literacy instruction
    c. they engage their students in intellectual discovery
    d. both a and c above

3. A teacher who encourages students to debate issues in the classroom is demonstrating a strength in: (p. 10)
    a. quality of instruction
    b. attitude toward subject
    c. attitude toward self
    d. all of the above

4. According to the 1992 NAEP study, which of the following groups scored highest on 4th grade achievement tests? (p. 11)
    a. Latinos
    b. Rural children
    c. Asian/Pacific Islander Children
    d. none of the above

5. According to the NAEP study, which reading approach was most widely favored by teachers? (p.11)
    a. whole language
    b. literature based
    c. basal
    d. silent reading

6. According to the NAEP study, what is the relationship between students' interest in reading and their age? (p. 12)
    a. students read more as they get older
    b. students don't like to read when they are young
    c. students read less as they get older
    d. both a and b above

7.   According to the NAEP study, what is the relationship between kinds of reading practices in the home and students' reading proficiency? (p. 13)
    a. students who had access to reading materials at home had higher proficiency
    b. students from wealthier families had the highest proficiency
    c. both a and b above
    d. no relationship was found

8.   The NAEP study and a previous study by Langer, Applebee, Mullis, and Foertsch (1980) found that in most classrooms: (p. 13)
    a. there is no integration of reading and writing
    b. emphasis on worksheets is being replaced by discussion groups
    c. higher level reasoning is not emphasized enough
    d. both a and b above

9.   The results of a 1991 report from the Select Committee on Children, Youth, and Families suggest that almost half of children today: (p. 11)
    a. have developmental disabilities
    b. live in homes with only one parent
    c. are at-risk of failing in school
    d. none of the above

10.   An understanding of the relationship between theory and practice is: (p. 5)
    a. important because we operate on the basis of our assumptions about teaching, learning, and children
    b. rarely required in public school teaching
    c. not as important as having a knowledge of instructional methods in teaching
    d. a and b above

<u>Answers to Multiple Choice Items</u>
1. a
2. d
3. d
4. c
5. b
6. c
7. a
8. c
9. c
10. a

<u>Notes:</u>

Chapter 2. Coming to Know the Reading and Writing Processes:
Understanding Meaning Making

Chapter Summary

This chapter, "Coming to Know the Reading and Writing Processes: Understanding Meaning Making," introduces students to language and literacy processes. The development of language background knowledge in the preschool and elementary school years is emphasized. Central to the chapter is the understanding of reading as an interactive meaning construction process which directly involves the reader's previous experience and background knowledge. The importance of reader motivation, reading comprehension strategies, and meaning monitoring strategies in comprehending and using printed text are also emphasized.

Teaching Suggestions

1. Use the Double Entry Journal (DEJ), on "things you do as you read and write" and "your own literacy history," in small and large group discussions.

2. To introduce this chapter present "The Wimmy Wuggen and the Moggy Tor" (p. 30) through an oral reading followed by the four questions (p. 31). Discuss the key insights related to the reading process (p. 31-32). Develop an overhead transparency for BLM 2-1, Six Key Components of Expert Reader Competencies, (text p. 33) and use this to synthesize your discussion.

3. Identify one or more cartoons (Gary Larson's "The Far Side" cartoons work particularly well). Make a transparency of the cartoon(s) and project the image on a white screen. Have students work in small groups to (a) choose one cartoon, (b) identify and list all schemata needed to "get" the cartoon, and (c) discuss how background knowledge schema influence understanding humor, especially for students who speak English as a Second Language. Lead a large group discussion of the groups' conclusions.

4. Ask students to reexamine Sarah's (Age 5) and Matt's (Age 6) uninterrupted writing samples and illustrations (Figure 2-1, p. 39 of the text) and to interpret their invented spelling text. The illustrations should be used to assist this interpretation. (Sarah: "Once upon a time there was a lovable bunny who picked a rose for his mommy." Matt: "I like to go to the zoo. I like to have lunch there. I like the zebras.") Explore the classification of each of these responses based on the classroom functions using an overhead transparency for BLM 2-2, Classroom Language Functions, (text p. 47). Explore the question, "What role does invented spelling play in children's emergent literacy.

5. As a class assignment ask your students to bring to class a written
    statement of their personal insights on the topic of "My Definition of the
    Reading and Writing Processes" (two to three pages). Encourage them to
    account for the role of comprehension as well as attitudes and motivation
    in their definition. Provide opportunity for students to share their
    definitions with a class partner or small group. Following the discussion
    ask them to make notes on new ideas that they believe should be included
    in their definitions. Finally, ask students to keep their definitions in a
    convenient location in their notebooks and to add new ideas to the
    definition as they progress through your course. We ask our students to
    revise their definitions at mid point and at the conclusion of the course.
    Your feedback to these revisions will provide important insight into your
    students' constructions of meaning and will assist in developing their
    understanding of the reading and writing processes.

Black Line Masters (BLM) for Chapter 2

> BLM 2-1 (text p. 33) Six Key Components of Expert Reader Competencies
> BLM 2-2 (text p. 47) Classroom Language Functions
> BLM 2-3 (text p. 60) The Meaning Construction Process - Meaning
>   Negotiation Between Teacher and Child

Evaluation Options

1. Your observations of student participation in small and large group
    discussions.

2. Your reading and evaluative response to "My Definition of the Reading and
    Writing Processes" (see #5 above).

3. Your evaluation of student responses to Short Answer Essay Questions (see
    items below). Please note that we have provided page numbers that are
    keyed to the text indicating where the content related to each question is
    located. You may wish to use these questions as a study guide for you
    students rather than as an evaluation option.

4. Your evaluation of Multiple Choice Questions (see items below). Again, you
    will find each question is keyed to the text content and you may wish to
    use these questions as a study guide.

5. Your evaluation of students' portfolios.

Short Answer Essay Questions

1. Of the six components of expert reader competencies listed on page 33 of your text, identify two you believe to be most important and explain why. (p. 33)

2. Explain why an understanding of emergent literacy is crucial for the beginning stages of reading and writing instruction. (p. 38)

3. What is a schema and what role does schema theory play in reading comprehension? (pp. 52-53)

4. Briefly explain the role of social interaction in literacy development. (pp. 37-61)

Multiple Choice Questions

1. Studies indicate that language processing ability begins at: (p.29)
   a. birth
   b. 18 months of age
   c. 3 years of age
   d. none of the above

2. Children's control over syntactic structures: (p. 35)
   a. is complete by age 5
   b. begins at age 5
   c. extends into the elementary school years
   d. both b and c above

3. Which of the following best describes the difference between Piaget's theory and Vygotsky's theory? (pp. 36-37)
   a. Piaget discusses stages of cognitive development while Vygotsky focuses on the social interactions of children with peers and adults
   b. Vygotsky's zone of proximal development is not mentioned in Piaget's work
   c. Vygotsky's theory is based on language while Piaget's is not
   d. both a and b above

4. According to Haggard's study (1980,) what is the strongest motivating factor in acquiring new vocabulary for young children? (p. 37)
   a. the sound of the word
   b. the frequency of the new word's occurrence in children's stories
   c. social interaction
   d. none of the above

5. Which of the following is not a characteristic of invented spelling? (p. 40)
   a. it is systematic
   b. it is rule-governed
   c. children only invent spellings in kindergarten and first grade
   d. it is consistent in nature

6. Studies have examined the relationship between home influences and language growth and have found that: (p. 44)
   a. poor children have limited language use
   b. language patterns from middle class families closely match those used in school
   c. minority children aren't very verbal
   d. all of the above

7. Which of the following is characteristic of dialects? (p.50)
    a. they are irregular language systems
    b. they interfere with learning to such an extent that they should be eliminated
    c. they are rule governed
    d. both a and b above

8. How does content reading differ from story reading? (p. 51)
    a. the text structure differs
    b. content reading involves more prediction
    c. content reading includes more narratives
    d. both a and b above

9. Which of the following is an example of metacognition? (p. 57)
    a. self-monitoring as we read
    b. reciting the alphabet
    c. automatic word recognition
    d. none of the above

10. Which of the following has the greatest influence on the development of background schema? (p. 54)
    a. cognition
    b. social interaction
    c. vocabulary knowledge
    d. both a and b above

1. a
2. c
3. d
4. a
5. c
6. b
7. c
8. a
9. a
10.d

Notes:

Chapter 3. Understanding the Beginning Steps: Early Reading and Writing Development

Chapter Summary

Chapter 3, "Understanding the Beginning Steps: Early Reading and Literacy Development," addresses emergent and early reading and writing. The view of children as experienced information-seekers, theory builders, and hypothesis-testers is central from the very beginning of the chapter, and all that follows in congruent with that view. The chapter examines characteristics of classrooms that facilitate children's language and literacy development, explores issues of meaning negotiation in classrooms, examines patterns of children's early language and literacy development, and presents instructional activities and strategies for guiding children's early literacy development.

Instructional strategies are introduced for developing children's understanding of the language of instruction and concepts about literacy, guiding group participation, developing picture and print awareness, guiding early writing and spelling, developing children's sense of story and narrative, and building positive attitudes. Included also are informal reading and literacy assessment strategies. Specific activities range from the use of language experience charts and big books to shared book experiences and the Directed Listening-Thinking Activity (DL-TA).

Teaching Suggestions

1. Have students work in small groups to discuss the results of their DEJ thinking about what children need to know to learn how to read and write and what we can <u>teach</u> them about reading and writing. Have the groups report out in full class discussion.

2. Demonstrate the Language-Experience Approach using a "fishbowl" activity in which a small group demonstrates an activity while the rest of the class observes. Bring an object or picture to class that will stimulate animated discussion. Select a small group of students to be in the fishbowl. Emphasize that you are <u>not asking them to role-play as kindergarten or first-grade children</u>; rather, you will initiate and carry out an adult simulation of the L-EA. Gather the small group students' chairs and yours in a place in the classroom where you have access to a chalkboard with the rest of the class arranged around the fishbowl group in such a way that observation of the group is easily done. Introduce your object or picture and encourage discussion of it. At an appropriate time ask, "What would you like to write about our _____?" and begin recording students' responses <u>exactly as they are given</u>. When finished, read the account back to the students and ask, "Are there any changes you would like to make?" Guide discussion of revisions and then announce that this is our final account. Read the account aloud again inviting fishbowl members to read

along with you. At the appropriate time, stop the simulation and open a debriefing discussion with the entire class. Debriefings are productively initiated by asking any or all of the following questions: "What was going on in this lesson?" "What were the children doing?" "What was the teacher doing?" "What language interactions and transactions were going on?" Note that students will be responding from two different viewpoints - those who observed the simulation and those who experienced it. Continue guiding discussion as needed. You may wish to connect this discussion with the Conditions for Optimal Learning on page 73 of the text.

3. Demonstrate a Directed Listening-Thinking Activity using an adult short story or the opening chapter of a novel. This can easily be done with the whole class. In advance, select your stop-points and think about your questions. After the DL-TA debrief in much the same way you did after the L-EA simulation. Call students' attention to the DL-TA HOW TO DO on p. 114 and the BUILDING TABLE on p. 133.

4. Prepare BLM 3-3, Developing a Lesson Plan, as both a handout and an overhead transparency. Depending on the experience level of your students, spend some time discussing lesson planning, specifically with regard to the concepts developed in this chapter. Assign students the task of creating a DL-TA lesson plan for kindergarten or first grade. You may wish to use the form provided in BLM 3-3 or, alternatively, a form used in your program.

5. Prepare BLM 3-2, Observational Checklist, (text pp. 123-124) as both a handout and overhead transparency. Walk through the checklist item noting how and when in the L-EA and DL-TA simulations information for each item was apparent. Encourage students to use the checklist in one or more observations of emergent and early readers and writers.

Black Line Masters (BLM) for Chapter 3

BLM 3-1 (text p. 76) Meaning Negotiation in Classroom Interaction Using Personal, Group, Text, and Task Meanings
BLM 3-2 (text pp. 123-124) Observational Checklist - Emergent and Early Readers and Writers
BLM 3-3 (not in text) Developing a Lesson Plan, 5pp.

Evaluation Options

1. Your observations of student participation in small and large groups.

2. Your evaluation of students' lesson plans (see #s 3 and 4 above).

3. Your evaluation of student responses to Short Answer Essay Questions (see items below). Please note that we have provided page numbers that are

keyed to the text indicating where the content related to each question is located. You may wish to use these questions as a study guide for your students rather than as an evaluation option.

4. Your evaluation of Multiple Choice Questions (see items below). Again, you will find each questions is keyed to the text content and you may wish to use these questions as a study guide.

5. Your evaluation of students' portfolios.

Short Answer Essay Questions

1. In Cambourne's discussion of the seven conditions for optimal learning, why is "approximation" important for the development of early literacy? (p. 73)

2. Discuss one instructional goal for early literacy instruction and at least two activities you feel would be appropriate for implementing this goal. (p. 33)

3. Explain how a Directed Listening-Thinking activity contributes to the understanding of narrative text and comprehension development. (p.111)

4. Briefly discuss how you would organize your reading center to encourage high motivation for your students. (p. 115)

Multiple Choice Questions

1. According to Doyle and Carter, in the face of ambiguity and risk, children: (pp.77-78)
    a. construct their own definitions of the task
    b. ask questions to reduce ambiguity
    c. may refuse to work until more information is forthcoming
    d. all of the above

2. According to Pauline Harris, in negotiating meaning in the classroom, the child relies upon four types of meaning. An example of task meaning is: (p. 75)
    a. an understanding of story features
    b. an understanding of sociolinguistic language patterns in the classroom
    c. the children's background knowledge
    d. both a and b above

3. The development of classroom participation rules:(p. 87)
    a. should be done only after children can identify first grade sight words
    b. enhances the task meanings in the classroom
    c. is mostly important for children with attention deficits
    d. enhances the text meanings in the classroom

4. One of the best ways to encourage a child to construct his/her own theories about written language is: (p. 103)
    a. to encourage invented spelling
    b. to provide the child with the correct spellings when he/she asks for them
    c. to avoid teaching conventional spelling
    d. both a and c above

5. The DL-TA is primarily useful for: (p. 111)
    a. teaching children word and spelling patterns
    b. developing a sense of prediction
    c. developing a sense of story plot
    d. both b and c above

6. In order to ensure the success of story reading activities: (p. 118)
    a. allow the children to interact with the story, primarily after you have finished reading
    b. create an atmosphere of enjoyment
    c. change the time when you read at least twice a week to avoid boredom
    d. both a and b above

7. The main advantage of publisher-developed reading programs is that: (p. 119)
   a. they contain all of the materials you need for reading
   b. they save time by providing an array of materials from which you can choose in setting up your reading program
   c. the objectives have already been defined appropriately for your class
   d. all of the above

8. Which of the following is the most effective assessment for beginning reading? (p. 120)
   a. the Metropolitan Readiness Test
   b. observation notes of children's progress in the classroom
   c. a test of auditory and visual discrimination
   d. none of the above

9. An example of an appropriate observation in kindergarten is: (p. 123)
   a. noting the child's level of engagement while listening to stories
   b. noting how well the child can copy sentences
   c. counting the number of words the child can identify
   d. both a and c above

10. When doing a DL-TA, an appropriate question to ask after reading a segment of the story is: (pp. 111-114)
   a. What happened to the main character in that segment?
   b. Where does the story take place?
   c. What do you think will happen next?
   d. none of the above

Answers to Multiple Choice Items

1. d
2. b
3. b
4. a
5. d
6. b
7. b
8. b
9. b
10. c

Notes:

Chapter 4. Developing Reading Comprehension:
Using Instructional Strategies to Develop Higher-Level Thinking

Chapter Summary

This chapter explores various aspects of the comprehension process, including levels of thinking and questioning (factual, interpretive, applicative, and transactive), comprehension skills (identifying details, sequence of events, cause and effect, main idea, predicting outcomes, valuing, problem solving), and questioning and discussion strategies (focusing, extending, clarifying, raising, receiving, controlling, ignoring, wait time). The bulk of the chapter is spent demonstrating and discussing at length instructional strategies for guiding comprehension. The instructional strategies developed in this chapter are the Directed Reading-Thinking Activity (DR-TA), the Directed Reading Activity (DRA), the PreReading Plan (PReP), Question-Answer Relationships (QAR), the Reciprocal Questioning Activity (ReQuest), Reciprocal Teaching, and the Group Mapping Activity (GMA).

Teaching Suggestions

1. Prepare BLM 4-1, Levels of Thinking, (text p. 141) as an overhead transparency. Prepare handouts of a narrative story (or use multiple copies of texts or books you have) and distribute copies to students in small groups. Ask them to work as a group to write five questions for their text and be prepared to identify the level of thinking and comprehension skill addressed by each question. After groups are finished, use the overhead transparency to demonstrate each group's analysis of their questions. If you find that many of the questions are factual, guide discussion of ways to revise to move questions to higher levels.

2. Demonstrate the DR-TA in much the same way you did the DL-TA (Chapter 3) by selecting a short story or first chapter of an adult novel (using a chapter is an excellent way also to demonstrate how the DR-TA is useful in a literature-based approach). Prepare copies of the text as handouts and get blank sheets of paper for the coversheet. Preplan your stop-points and questions. Initiate your simulation by having students cover everything on the first page except the title (and author, if you wish). Ask, "With a title like that, what do you think this story will be about?" and follow up with "Why?" and "What makes you say that?" as students respond. If you're not an experienced DR-TA user, find a story that has suspense built in to it. Don't rush student responses; be willing to wait awhile for them to speak if you have to. Give the DR-TA magic time to happen - it will.

3. Follow the DR-TA with the Group Mapping Activity (GMA). Prepare in advance the "dummy" maps to use as you give instructions; you may wish to use BLMs 4-4 and 4-5, Sample Story Maps, (text pp. 190-191) or, alternately, create your own. A key issue here is for students to do their

maps <u>without looking back at the story</u>. Lead a discussion of map sharing - this is the really powerful part of the simulation and where much comprehension of the story takes place. Have students hold up their maps "so we can see how different they are" (expect giggles). Then ask, "Who'd like to share their map?" and wait for someone to volunteer. Then you model questioning that allows students to extend their thinking (e.g., "What made you decide to place your arrow in that position?" "Why did you choose to make Laura the center of your map?").

4.   After demonstrating the DR-TA and GMA lead a debriefing session in which students analyze what was going on in these instructional transactions ("What was the teacher doing?" "What were the students doing?"). Link students' insights to points in the text. Go back to the text and talk about DR-TA-type questions (text p. 158) and how these relate to levels of thinking; go over the key features of DR-TA (text pp. 158-159); walk through HOW TO DO for the DR-TA and GMA (text pp. 159 and 196, respectively) and check out each in the BUILDING TABLE (text pp. 204-205). Prepare BLM 4-6, 4-7, and 4-8, Carey's and Alita's Maps, (text pp. 193 & 195) as overhead transparencies for use during debriefing of GMA.

5.   Using multiple copies of children's books or stories, have student work in small groups to begin writing lesson plans using the DR-TA and GMA and/or any other of the instructional strategies presented in the chapter. Assign a DR-TA/GMA lesson plan to be handed in next week. Remind students they will need to provide a copy of the text in order for you to evaluate their choice of stop-points. Emphasize the open-ended nature of DR-TA-type questions. We encourage our students to actually try out their DR-TA/GMA lessons whenever possible so that they'll have a chance to see the lesson in action and reflect on it.

6.   End class by having students use their DEJ responses and all that has gone on in class to talk in small groups about all the things teachers need to do to guide full, rich comprehension of text.

<u>Black Line Masters (BLM) for Chapter 4</u>

BLM 4-1 (text p. 141) Levels of Thinking
BLM 4-2 (text p. 149) Story Discussion #1, <u>Alexander and the Windup Mouse</u>
BLM 4-3 (text p. 150) Story Discussion #2, <u>Alexander and the Windup Mouse</u>
BLM 4-4 (text p. 190) Sample Story Map
BLM 4-5 (text p. 191) Sample Story Map
BLM 4-6 (text p. 193) Carey's Map
BLM 4-7 (text p. 195) Alita's Map of <u>The Bears on Hemlock Mountain</u>
BLM 4-8 (text p. 195) Alita's Map of <u>Flibbity Jibbet and the Key Keeper</u>

<u>Evaluation Options</u>

1. Your observations of student participation in small and large group demonstrations and discussions.

2. Your evaluation of students' lesson plans (see #5 above).

3. Your evaluation of student responses to Short Answer Essay Questions (see items below). Please note that we have provided page numbers that are keyed to the text indicating where the content related to each question is located. You may wish to use these questions as a study guide for your students rather than as an evaluation option.

4. Your evaluation of Multiple Choice Questions (see items below). Again, you will find each questions is keyed to the text content and you may wish to use these questions as a study guide.

5. Your evaluation of students' portfolios.

Short Answer Questions

1. Why is it important to include interpretive, applicative, and transactive questions in developing comprehension? (pp. 143-144)

2. Explain how the comprehension skill of main idea could be used at each of the four levels of thinking, i.e. factual, interpretive, applicative, and transactive. (p. 145)

3. Select one of the following comprehension strategies, i.e. QAR, PReP, ReQuest,Reciprocal Teaching, or Group Mapping, and explain how this strategy could be used to develop thinking processes at the interpretive, applicative, and transactive levels. (pp. 171-196)

4. Why are the "clarifying" and "raising" questioning and discussion strategies critical for the development of comprehension? (p. 148)

Multiple Choice Questions

1. Various studies of teacher questioning strategies have found that: (p. 140)
    a. teachers usually do not use open-ended questions
    b. the strategies most teachers use help students to understand the complexity of the text
    c. most strategies used by teachers do not encourage higher level comprehension
    d. both a and c above

2. Which of the following comprehension questions related to this chapter illustrates the interpretive level of thinking? (p. 143)
    a. What are the four levels of thinking involved in comprehension?
    b. What is the relationship between motivation and reading comprehension?
    c. How might you use questioning strategies in your own teaching?
    d. both b and c above

3. Which of the following comprehension questions related to this chapter illustrates the applicative level? (p. 143)
    a. What are the four levels of thinking involved in comprehension?
    b. What is the relationship between motivation and reading comprehension?
    c. How might you use questioning strategies in your own teaching?
    d. none of the above

4. Oral reading is most appropriately done by the children: (p. 160)
    a. during a DR-TA for the purposes of enhancing comprehension
    b. after students have read the text silently during a DRA
    c. using a new text in a round robin fashion
    d. both b and c above

5. The DRA and the DR-TA both develop: (p. 171)
    a. high reader motivation
    b. high level comprehension skills
    c. high level thinking skills
    d. all of the above

6.	Suppose that you are using the PReP to activate the readers' background knowledge before reading this chapter. Which of the following responses to the question, "Tell me anything that comes to mind when you hear the term 'reading comprehension'," indicates that the reader has only some prior knowledge? (p. 173)
a. it has to do with understanding what you read
b. it means doing assignments in class
c. the activation of background knowledge, application of reading strategies, and higher level thinking when reading
d. none of the above

7.	Suppose that you are using the QAR strategy in discussing this chapter, which of the following is an example of an "Author and You" question?(p. 175)
a. What are the main components of the comprehension process?
b. What is the relationship between motivation and reading comprehension?
c. How might you use PReP strategies to introduce Charlotte's Web?
d. none of the above

8.	After reading a segment of Charlotte's Web, if you were to ask the students, "Why do you think Charlotte introduced herself to Wilbur?" you could be using: (pp. 175, 182)
a. a "think and search" question from the QAR procedure
b. part of the DR-TA procedure
c. a ReQuest strategy
d. both a and c above

9.	The Reciprocal Teaching Strategy, which emphasizes social interaction between student and teacher, is most closely related to which of the following theories discussed in Chapter 2? (pp. 184-188; pp. 36-37)
a. Piaget's theory
b. Vygotsky's theory
c. Chomsky's theory
d. both a and c

10	Which of the following is developed through group mapping? (pp. 189-196)
a. knowledge of syntactic structure
b. the ability to think metaphorically
c. an understanding of story sequence
d. both b and c above

<u>Answers to Multiple Choice Items</u>
1. c
2. b
3. c
4. b
5. d
6. a
7. c
8. d
9. b
10.d

<u>Notes:</u>

Chapter 5. Building Vocabulary and Comprehension Connections

Chapter Summary

Chapter 5, "Building Vocabulary Knowledge and Comprehension Connections," explores the complex relationship between vocabulary and comprehension. The chapter makes the case that a clear distinction should be drawn between vocabulary instruction that occurs before, during, or after reading in which before-reading instruction is aimed at short term recall of word meanings important to the comprehension of text, during-reading instruction is quick assistance for a student's immediate need of understanding, and after-reading instruction is focused on long-term retention of newly learned words. Guidelines are presented to assist your students in selecting new words to be taught and determining whether what vocabulary instruction is needed before, during, and after story or text reading. Emphasized throughout the chapter are strategies for teaching vocabulary in context, developing word meanings in relationship to known concepts and words, and in guiding children toward becoming independent word learners. Specific instructional strategies developed in this chapter are Teaching Vocabulary in Context (TVC), Context-Structure-Sound-Reference (CSSR), Vocabulary Self-Collection Strategy (VSS), Concept Webs, Semantic Mapping, Semantic Feature Analysis (SFA), and Vocabulary Logs and Journals.

Teaching Suggestions

1. Use the DEJ responses to start small group discussion of how your students process unknown words. Have groups report out in large group discussion.

2. Conduct a full-class discussion to clarify different purposes for vocabulary instruction and the distinctions between before-, during- and after-reading vocabulary instruction.

3. Demonstrate before-reading vocabulary instruction using adult level narrative and expository text so that you can find words that students do not already know (popular press magazines are good for this purpose). Prepare BLM 5-1, When You Come to a Word You Do Not Know, (text p.221) as an overhead transparency. Select five or six words from a text and write them on the board in the context of the sentence each is in; underline the target words. Project the When You Come to a Word You Do Not Know chart on a white screen or wall, and conduct a discussion of each target word following the CSSR progression. Refer students to the chart periodically. This demonstration allows you to simulate both the teaching of new words and the teaching of an independent process for learning new words. Debrief after the simulation. Walk students through the HOW TO DO (text p. 222) and the BUILDING TABLE (text pp. 252-253).

4.   Demonstrate after-reading vocabulary instruction using the Vocabulary Self-Collection Strategy (VSS). Have students bring to class (or you distribute once again) the story you used to teach DR-TA and GMA (Chapter 4). Have students work in small groups to do a VSS. Each group is to nominate two words or terms they want to learn or know more about (you will also nominate two words or terms); students are to tell 1) where they found the words/terms, 2) what they think each means, 3) why they want to learn or know more about each. Work all the way through the VSS allowing all groups to nominate, and nominate a word yourself. Narrow the list down as the class wishes, and develop class definition of each word or term. If students still have their maps with them from the GMA have them locate the VSS words on their maps. Debrief after the simulation and emphasize the importance of teacher-developed activities to follow-up and reinforce initial learning. Walk students through the HOW TO DO (text p. 225) and the building table (text pp. 252-253).

5.   To demonstrate follow-up activities, prepare in advance a Semantic Feature Analysis (SFA) using words from the same story you used to teach the DR-TA (BLM 5-3). After selecting the VSS words (see above) have students asterisk the VSS words that appear on the grid. Have them work in small groups to complete the SFA. Give them plenty of time for discussion, then lead a large class discussion of the activity. You can expect a certain amount of student discomfort, or even crankiness, from doing SFA. That's because the exercise itself is centered in <u>individual</u> interpretation that must be reconciled through discussion. Show students how to lead a class through the discomfort. Debrief and connect the strategy back to VSS.

6.   Assign two lesson plans: one for before-reading vocabulary instruction and one for after-reading vocabulary instruction. Encourage students to combine various instructional strategies.

<u>Black Line Masters (BLM) for Chapter 5</u>

BLM 5-1 (text pp. 221-222) When You Come to a Word You Do Not Know
BLM 5-2 (text p. 238) Semantic Feature Analysis for "Pets"
BLM 5-3 (not in text) Semantic Feature Analysis Grid

<u>Evaluation Options</u>

1.   Your observations of student participation in small and large group demonstrations and discussions.

2.   Your evaluation of students' lesson plans (see #6 above).

3.   Your evaluation of student responses to Short Answer Essay Questions (see items below). Please note that we have provided page numbers that are keyed to the text indicating where the content related to each question is

located. You may wish to use these questions as a study guide for your students rather than as an evaluation option.

4. Your evaluation of Multiple Choice Questions (see items below). Again, you will find each questions is keyed to the text content and you may wish to use these questions as a study guide.

5. Your evaluation of students' portfolios.

Short Answer Essay Questions

1. Why is it important for a teacher to be "context sensitive" when teaching vocabulary? (p. 212)

2. Discuss two strategies for helping a child to actively engage in learning vocabulary and provide at least one example from your own teaching for each strategy. (pp. 211-213)

3.Compare and contrast the nature and purpose of vocabulary instruction done "before," "during," and "after" reading a text. (pp. 215-216)

4. Choose a children's story and select three vocabulary items that you might teach. Discuss how you might use two of the following strategies in your vocabulary instruction: interactive cloze, synonyms, similes, concept webs, semantic maps.(226-236)

Multiple Choice Questions

1. If a child knows that "drive" has something to do with operating a car, but needs to know that "drive" can also mean to direct cattle toward a specific destination, your goal in teaching, according to Drum and Konopak, would be: (p. 211)
    a. to teach a new concept for an old label
    b. to teach a new label for an old concept
    c. to extend the attributes for a label
    d. none of the above

2. Novice teachers who begin to use the word "schema" in discussing reading comprehension with fellow teachers could be exemplifying: (pp.210-211, 214)
    a. one of Drum's and Konopak's states in learning word meanings
    b. one of Michael Grave's six vocabulary learning tasks
    c. one of Haggard's motivations for vocabulary learning
    d. all of the above

3. The decision as to when to introduce and develop new words in text material, i.e. before, during or after reading, depends upon: (p. 215)
    a. your beliefs about the importance of the words for understanding the story
    b. the background knowledge of your students
    c. how important you feel it is for the children to develop independence in vocabulary learning
    d. all of the above

4. The final selection of new vocabulary to be taught depends upon: (p. 216)
    a. the new vocabulary identified in the basal reader
    b. your children's familiarity with the story content
    c. the extent to which the text is "friendly" or "unfriendly"
    d. both b and c above

5. If the teacher asks students to nominate words that they would like to learn more about, she is demonstrating: (p. 223)
    a. the VSS
    b. the CSSR system
    c. vocabulary instruction done before reading the text
    d. both a and c above

6. One of the main advantages of the Vocabulary Self-Collection strategy is that: (pp.224-226)
      a. it increases motivation to learn new words
      b. it ensures that the children know the words before they read the text
      c. it can be used with a variety of materials
      d. both a and c above

7. The main difference between concept maps and semantic maps is that: (pp. 230-237)
      a. only semantic maps are graphic representations
      b. only concept maps are based upon a central concept in the story
      c. only semantic maps show relationships among concepts and key ideas in the text
      d. brainstorming is done only with a concept map

8. If you were to list the major characters of a story the children have read and then ask the children to brainstorm some adjectives which describe the emotions of the characters, you could use these two lists to formulate: (pp.230-231; 237-240)
      a. semantic maps
      b. a semantic feature analysis
      c. concept maps
      d. all of the above

9. Teaching that some words, like the word "mosquito," are borrowed from another language, is important: (pp. 243-344)
      a. for increasing children's interest in learning new vocabulary
      b. for encouraging children to explore the origins of words
      c. because it will motivate children to understand different cultures
      d. all of the above

10. Vocabulary and reading comprehension are related because: (pp.207-209)
      a. children's proficiency in both is related to their socioeconomic level
      b. vocabulary knowledge is essential for successful reading comprehension
      c. the role of background knowledge is important in the development of both
      d. both b and c above

Answers to Multiple Choice Items

1. a
2. d
3. d
4. d
5. a
6. d
7. c
8. d
9. d
10 d

Notes:

Chapter 6. Using Literature and Reader Response to Enhance Attitudes and Comprehension

Chapter Summary

Chapter 6, "Using Literature and Reader Response to Enhance Attitudes and Comprehension," introduces your students to children's literature and the importance of reader response as the catalyst for children's continuing desire to read. The use of an aesthetic instructional stance designed to build internal reader motivation, such as intellectual curiosity and self-understanding, is emphasized.

This chapter develops an understanding of how to select high interest children's literature and organize the classroom literature and reading center. Specific instructional strategies presented include Reading Aloud, Story Telling, Reader Response and Literature Response Journals, Sharing Responses About Books, Sustained Silent Reading (SSR), Readers Theatre, the Investigative Questioning Procedure (InQuest), and Thematic Units. The informal evaluation of children's progress in responding to literature is emphasized.

The important role of children's literature in the elementary grade reading program will become clear to your students as they understand the nature of reader motivation and reader response. This discussion is especially important in light of the many state and local literature initiatives which have developed throughout the country.

Teaching Suggestions

1.   Ask students to complete the following written assignment (2 to 3 pages). First, ask each student reflect on the books they have read ranging from the earliest experiences with children's literature to reading in adult life. Second, have each student identify one influential book (there in all probability will be several) that has had a major impact on his or her life at the time the book was read and briefly describe the nature of this impact. Finally, they are to identify the internal (pp. 263-265) and external (pp. 265-266) motivations that were critical in this influence. Provide time for your students to share their written responses and ideas in a small group of three to five students. Have each group nominate one student's response to be shared with the total class. Summarize and synthesize the discussion by listing each nominated book on the chalk board and identifying the key internal and external motivations. Provide an evaluative response to the written assignment.

2.   Complete the same influential book assignment described in #1 above. Ask each student to reflect on the three step reader motivation and response process of identification, catharsis, and insight (pp. 259-260) that was involved in reading her or his favorite book (see pp. 256-257 for an actual

example from Pat Durkum for <u>Little House on the Prairie</u>). Have your students share their ideas in partner teams or in small groups. Now with your total class explore the relationship between a child's prior knowledge and experience with books and the identification and motivation process.

3. Explore the role of instructional stance in helping students establish a reading purpose and motivation to read. Take a number of children's literature selections to class. For example, books highly appropriate for this exercise are those such as Maurice Sendak's <u>Where the Wild Things Are</u>, Virginia Hamilton's <u>The People Could Fly</u>, Herb Kane's <u>Pele Goddess of Hawaii's Vocanoes</u>, Ruth Heller's <u>Plants that Never Bloom</u>, Whitfield's <u>Why Do Volcanoes Erupt</u>?, E.B. White's <u>Charlotte's Web</u>, and Wildlife Education books such as <u>Zoo Books: Wolves</u>. After discussing the aesthetic and efferent stances divide your class into small groups and distribute samples of each type of book to each of the student groups. Ask the students to explore the instructional stance they would take in developing a selected book with their students and to explain why they chose that stance. Encourage them to consider how they might use one particular book from both an efferent and an aesthetic stance. Finally, have the students develop several discussion questions that would illustrate both efferent and aesthetic stances (see pp. 261-262 for aesthetic stance question prompts; see pp. 262 for efferent stance question prompts). Prepare handout copies of BLM 6-3, The Newberry Medal Award Books, BLM 6-4, the Caldecott Medal Award Books, and BLM 6-5, Kids' Favorite Books: Children's Choices, to give your students' additional resources for locating good books.

4. Duplicate copies of a short story that has a number of characters and lots of interesting dialog. Distribute copies to the class and ask for volunteers to participate in a readers theatre reading of the story. After selecting a student for each character and a narrator give the rest of the class a partnership or small group discussion task (see #3 above) and work with the readers theatre group to guide their preparation. Provide highlight markers and suggest that the group use them for each person to mark her or his speaking parts. Discourage reliance on props or physical acting; readers theatre is intended to be much like a radio play where all of the "acting" is done with the voice. Recommend that in their practice they work on timing so that speaking parts follow narration smoothly. Give the group time for practice and then have them perform for the class. Have the audience take notes and jot down comments as the play progresses. Debrief the process making sure that the performing group gets to talk about what they did in preparation and that everyone talks about how the teacher prepared the group to work. An alternative here is to provide sufficient duplicated stories for everyone to work in a group and perform their story.

5. Lead a discussion with your class on evaluating children's progress in

responding to literature. Initiate this discussion by refocusing on the goals (p. 257) and objectives (p. 258) of a literature program. Through small group discussions encourage your students to create an evaluation plan in the form of observation questions that will form a checklist to provide information on children's attitude, motivation, and response to literature. After they have created their plan and related questions ask them to turn to p. 297 and compare their questions with those found in the section on "Evaluating Children's Progress in Responding to Literature." Ask you students to add any additional ideas found there that will enhance their checklist of questions.

Black Line Masters for Chapter 6

BLM 6-1 (text p. 274) Teachers' Favorite Books for Classroom Reading Center

BLM 6-2 (text p. 295) Second-Grade Topical Thematic Literature Unit on Foxes

BLM 6-3 (not in text) The Newberry Medal Award Books, 3pp.

BLM 6-4 (not in text) The Caldecott Medal Award Books, 3pp.

BLM 6-5 (not in text) Kids' Favorite Books: Children's Choices, 4 pp.

Evaluation Options

1. Your observations of student participation in small and large group discussions.

2. Your reading and evaluative response to suggestion #1 above.

3. Your evaluation of student responses to Short Answer Essay Questions (see items below). Please note that we have provided page numbers that are keyed to the text indicating where the content related to each question is located. You may wish to use these questions as a study guide for you students rather than as an evaluation option.

4. Your evaluation of Multiple Choice Questions (see items below). Again, you will find each question is keyed to the text content and you may wish to use these questions as a study guide.

5. Your evaluation of students' portfolios.

Short Answer Essay Questions

1. Choose a book from those that you have most recently read. Identify your predominant stance in reading this book and explain why you read from this stance. What were the main internal reader motivations that applied to your reading of this book?
(pp. 260-265)

2. Choose a children's book and write two discussion questions about the book which illustrate a predominantly aesthetic stance in your instruction. Write two questions, based on the same book, illustrating a predominantly efferent stance.
(p. 261-262)

3. Choose a children's book and discuss for what grade level(s) you feel it is most appropriate. Explain your rationale. (pp. 267-268)

4. Discuss how you would organize a reading center at the grade level of greatest interest to you. Explain how your choice of materials and their location would contribute to high interest voluntary reading and your instructional goals. (pp. 272-273)

Multiple Choice Questions

1. In discussing the book <u>Charlotte's Web,</u> the question, "What do you know about spiders?" is an example of:(pp. 261-262)
    a. a way to evoke prior knowledge
    b. a question which prompts the aesthetic stance
    c. a question which prompts the efferent stance
    d. both a and c above

2. A teacher who uses a predominantly aesthetic stance in his/her instruction: (p. 262)
    a. should focus more attention on content
    b. is helping to develop children's positive attitudes towards reading
    c. will frequently ask questions such as, "What idea did you find interesting in this book?"
    d. both b and c above

3. A teacher can take a predominantly efferent instructional stance: (p. 262-263)
    a. with expository text
    b. with narrative text
    c. with non-fiction books
    d. any of the above

4. Children's own jump rope rhymes: (p. 272)
    a. should only be used in the early grades
    b. are a form of poetry
    c. can be a form of multicultural instruction
    d. both b and c above

5. A child who writes in his/her response journal, "One of the events in this chapter reminded me of something that happened to me last year," is demonstrating: (p. 284)
    a. a character interaction response
    b. a prediction and validation response
    c. a personal experience response
    d. both a and c above

6. The main difference between writing a book report and book sharing is: (pp. 284-285)
    a. only book reports involve writing
    b. assigning book reports will ensure that the children actually read the book
    c. book sharing involves a number of options for actively involving children in literature
    d. both b and c above

7. If students persist in talking during SSR, the teacher should: (p. 288)
    a. encourage children to whisper responses to a partner
    b. begin a point system for good behavior
    c. ignore the children who are talking
    d. require a written response after SSR

8. Readers Theatre is best used: (pp. 288-290)
    a. before children are fluent readers
    b. with costumes and props
    c. to create interest in a story
    d. both a and c above

9. In evaluating students' progress in responding to literature, the teacher should: (p. 297)
    a. note how often the children select books from the library
    b. observe their level of enjoyment when listening to stories
    c. observe whether or not the children are selecting books independently
    d. all of the above

10. Which of the following allows for the greatest variety of options with regard to comprehension, vocabulary, and literature response strategies? (p. 308-309)
    a. response journals
    b. thematic units
    c. readers theatre
    d. storytelling

Answers to Multiple Choice Items
1. d
2. b
3. d
4. d
5. d
6. c
7. a
8. c
9. d
10.b

Notes:

Chapter 7. Guiding Children's Writing

Chapter Summary

Chapter 7, "Guiding Children's Writing," explores children's writing development from their very early writing experiences through writing experiences and instruction in elementary school. The chapter presents a process writing approach and discusses at length how to implement the writing workshop and project-based or theme cycle-based writing. The chapter also addresses instructional issues regarding children's spelling and handwriting development.

Teaching Suggestions

1.   Have students in small groups respond to the DEJ prompts. Encourage students to bring to class any writing they have in process or completed that they'd like to share in their small group discussion. Emphasize the powerful impact teachers' sharing of their own writing has on children.

2.   Prepare an overhead transparency for BLM 7-1, "Andrew and the Painted House," (text pp. 322-323). Using the transparency discuss possible mini-lessons it might suggest. Demonstrate a mini-lesson from this story. After the mini-lesson debrief on the process.

3.   Prepare writing prompts for a map students created from one of the stories the class has previously read. Have students write from the prompts and share their writing in small groups. You may wish to extend this lesson by the following:

      "After everyone in your group has shared his or her writing spend some time making plans for how you'll take this writing further. What do you want to do with it? What, if any, additional resources do you need? Share your plans with your group."

      Debrief the process emphasizing how mapping assists students in organizing their thinking for writing.

4.   Prepare overhead transparencies and handouts for BLM 7-2, Status-of-the-Class Record Form, (text p. 338); BLM 7-3, Work Accomplished Form, (referred to in text p. 344); and BLM 7-4, Writing Skills Record Form, (referred to in text p. 345). Project the transparencies and lead discussions on how each is used. Distribute handouts and encourage students to duplicate and use the forms as they implement writing workshop.

5.   Demonstrate the opening activity for a project-based or theme cycle unit. You might want to do this by asking the class "What have you been thinking about lately? What's important to you right now?" Have them work in

small groups to produce a list of three timely and important issues. In large group collect all the small group issues by writing them on the board. Lead a discussion and winnowing-down process in which the class either (a) agrees on one issue it wants to study, or (b) agrees on what issue each group will study. Then in small groups have students work to answer the following: "What do you already know about your topic? What do you want to know? What resources appear to be likely good places to start getting information? What will be your next steps?" Debrief the process and demonstrate on the overhead transparency (BLM 7-2) status-of-the-class record keeping.

6. Have students add a writing component to a previously developed lesson plan or create a new lesson plan focusing on process writing and/or project-based or theme cycle units.

7. Point out HOW TO DO and BUILDING TABLE information for each strategy.

Black Line Masters (BLM) for Chapter 7

BLM 7-1 (text pp. 322-323) "Andrew and the Painted House," 2 pp.
BLM 7-2 (text p. 338) Status-of-the-Class Record Form
BLM 7-3 (referred to in text p. 344) Work Accomplished Form
BLM 7-4 (referred to in text p. 345) Writing Skills Record Form

Evaluation Options

1. Your observations of student participation in small and large group demonstrations and discussions.

2. Your evaluation of students' lesson plans (see #6 above).

3. Your evaluation of student responses to Short Answer Essay Questions (see items below). Please note that we have provided page numbers that are keyed to the text indicating where the content related to each question is located. You may wish to use these questions as a study guide for your students rather than as an evaluation option.

4. Your evaluation of Multiple Choice Questions (see items below). Again, you will find each questions is keyed to the text content and you may wish to use these questions as a study guide.

5. Your evaluation of students' portfolios.

<u>Short Answer Essay Questions</u>

1. Discuss the relationship between the drawings and scribbling of pre-school children and their later conventional writing. (p. 316)

2. Explain the importance of Vygotsky's theory in the development of writing. (pp. 325-329)

3. Choose two of Cambourne's conditions for optimal literacy learning from Chapter 3 and discuss how writers' workshop fulfills these conditions. (pp. 73-74; 329-349)

4.Explain how one might combine ideas from project-based writing with those in Chapter 6, on thematic units integrating literature and the content areas, to develop a theme cycle in the classroom.
(pp. 292-297; 350-353)

Multiple Choice Questions

1. Children's first attempts at writing:(pp. 313-314, 353)
   a. begin before a child enters school
   b. often consist of "scribbling"
   c. are usually "prephonemic"
   d. all of the above

2. In order for low SES children to successfully develop their writing, teachers should: (p. 314)
   a. provide remedial instruction for them at once
   b. help them overcome earlier deficits caused by lack of language experiences
   c. recognize that the home language and literacy experiences of these children may differ from those at school
   d. discuss the deficiencies of these children with their parents

3. Drawing is an important antecedent to writing because: (p. 316)
   a. art is symbolic
   b. drawing may contain some conventional writing forms
   c. stories are often represented in drawings
   d. all of the above

4. According to recent research on children's writing development: (pp 323-325)
   a. children use patterns that reflect their hypotheses about written language
   b. children pass through a series of clearly defined developmental stages
   c. children vary in the order in which they discover the conventions of written language
   d. both a and b above

5. Invented spellings: (p. 329)
   a. should be discouraged after second grade
   b. allow students to test out their hypotheses
   c. usually disappear when children are provided with appropriate models
   d. both b and c above

6. In setting up the writing workshop, a teacher should (pp. 329-334, 347))
   a. allow children plenty of choice in deciding when they want to write
   b. modify the structure as needed
   c. begin with bright marking pens to motivate students
   d. all of the above

7.   Mini-lessons are useful for: (p. 334-337)
         a. establishing procedures
         b. providing instruction in writing conventions
         c. discussing the content of students' writing
         d. all of the above

8.   An appropriate question to ask during a "honeybee" conference with a child during writing workshop is: (pp. 337-341)
         a. What are you writing about?
         b. How could you make this statement more descriptive?
         c. Is all this information important to your reader??
         d. all of the above

9.   In evaluating children's writing, it is important: (pp. 343-345)
         a. that some form of self-evaluation be used
         b. to choose at least two pieces of the children's best writing for
             inclusion in their portfolios
         c. to develop criteria that allow for comparisons among children
         d. both a and b above

10.   The sentence "Wien he wes dien the house.wes mise to." (When he was done, the house was messy too) taken from Ryan's story, "Andrew and the Painted House," in Figure 7-7, on page 322 of the text, represents which of the following spelling patterns? (pp. 40; 353)
         a. phonemic
         b. letter-name
         c. transitional
         d. derivational

<u>Answers to Multiple Choice Items</u>
1. d
2. c
3. d
4. a
5. d
6. b
7. d
8. a
9. a
10.b

<u>Notes:</u>

Chapter 8. Using Word Analysis Strategies to Develop Reader Independence: Transforming Print to Meaning

Chapter Summary

Chapter 8, "Using Word Analysis Strategies to Develop Reader Independence: Transforming Print to Meaning," builds your students' understanding of word analysis skill strategies essential for the elementary grades. The effective, and eventually automatic, use of letter-sound correspondences, letter patterns, syllable units and context clues is critical for children's rapid and independent reading. Discussion stresses the importance of reading instruction that introduces word analysis skills in a natural print context that provides children immediate feedback and check for meaning.

Understanding the content of this chapter is important to all your students, those who will use a basal reader anthology approach that has sequenced word analysis skills and prewritten instructional activities as well as those students who will have the opportunity and freedom to design and tailor their own word analysis program using a literature-based or whole language instructional approach. Critical here is not that they expect to move children through published word analysis programs, but rather that they have a deep understanding of the word analysis learning that children do, whether this learning comes from children's own explorations of language or from instruction.

Teaching Suggestions

1. Use the Double Entry Journal (DEJ), on "what you know and associations you have with phonics, phonics instruction, and word analysis skills," and "information useful (and not useful) for teaching reading" in small and large group discussions.

2. An effective way to introduce this is chapter is to ask your students to turn to the New Alphabet and the Dennis the Menace cartoon found on page 371. Ask them to use the New Alphabet to interpret the caption for the cartoon, to do this as quickly as possible (without turning the page for the answer), and to raise their hands when they are finished. Place half-minute time intervals on the chalkboard as students are reading, e.g., .30, 1, 1.30, 2, 2.30, 3, 3.30, 4, and record the number of students that complete the interpretation within each time interval. The objective here is to recreate a sense of the word analysis process that early readers encounter by using a new alphabet. After all students have completed the interpretation discuss the reasons for the range of individual time completion differences across the one-half minute time intervals. Then ask your students to become introspective and reflect on the word analysis strategies they used. Summarize the strategies identified on the chalkboard. Compare these to those discussed on pages 371 and 372 in the text. Summarize the discussion by emphasizing the range of word analysis strategies that are

essential to beginning and skilled reading. Prepare an overhead transparency for BLM 8-1, Strategies Used in Reading Using New Alphabet, (text pp. 371-372). (Note: You will find that this activity works well even though your students have previously read this chapter in preparing for class discussion.)

3.   Set up a role playing situation in which you assume the role of parent or education critic and your students assume the role of a classroom teacher. Present the following statement to your students and assume the parent or critic role: "Phonics isn't being taught, especially like it was years ago, and that's why kids can't read today" (see discussion on pp. 373-378 of the text). Direct this discussion to examine why this viewpoint is often held by the news media and some educational critics (The discussion on pp. 373-378 of the text, "Word Analysis and Phonics: A History of Controversy," will provide key ideas for emphasis.).

4.   Develop a classroom observation assignment for your students, preferably in kindergarten or first grade, to focus on the four stages of word analysis development. Before visiting the classroom encourage students to review our discussion of the characteristics of the four stages of word analysis development (pp. 378-380, logographic, transitional, alphabetic, orthographic). Ask them to observe a single student or a small group of students during their visit. Their objective is to identify the developmental level(s) of the student(s) based on the four categories and to briefly describe word analysis examples from their observations that support their conclusions (one to two pages).

5.   Ask you students to assume for the moment that a computer software company has asked them to develop sample materials for a first grade reading program. Divide your students into small working groups of four or five members each. Present the following problem and provide 20 to 30 minutes for discussion.

"A computer software company has asked you to develop a brief proposal containing the following information:

a)   Identify the first six letters you would use in your program and briefly explain your rationale for selecting these;
b)   Create a beginning vocabulary using these letters;
c)   Write a brief story using this vocabulary adding simple illustrations if necessary;
d)   Indicate what word analysis skills you would teach from the story."

After the student groups have developed their responses ask each group to place the letters, beginning vocabulary, and story on the chalkboard and briefly develop the proposal. (If time is short you may limit the presentations to two or three groups.) Discuss the ideas and rationale presented. (You will find the discussion on p. 404-405, "Suggestions for Instructional Sequence: Consonants," and "Sequencing Vowels" helpful in this discussion.) Use this discussion to review the "Goals and Objectives of World Analysis Instruction," found on pp. 380-381. Specific attention should be given to developing word analysis concepts in a meaning based context.

Black Line Masters (BLM) for Chapter 8

BLM 8-1 (text pp. 371-372 Strategies Used in Reading Using New Alphabet
BLM 8-2 (text p. 382) General Learning Order and Placement of Word
    Analysis Skills

Evaluation Options

1. Your observations of student participation in small and large group discussions.

2. Your reading and evaluative response to the classroom observational paper (see #4 above).

3. Your evaluation of student responses to Short Answer Essay Questions (see items below). Please note that we have provided page numbers that are keyed to the text indicating where the content related to each question is located. You may wish to use these questions as a study guide for you students rather than as an evaluation option.

4. Your evaluation of Multiple Choice Questions (see items below). Again, you will find each question is keyed to the text content and you may wish to use these questions as a study guide.

5. Your evaluation of students' portfolios.

1. Explain how a "top down" approach to reading instruction might differ from a "bottom up" approach.(p. 372; also see pp. 609-610)

2. Choose one of Ehri's four developmental stages of word recognition and discuss what word analysis skills could be most appropriately taught at that stage. Provide an example of one activity you would use to teach a skill at this level. (pp. 378-381; 385-422)

3. Compare and contrast word analysis instruction in a literature-based (or whole language) classroom with that in a classroom where basals are predominantly used. (pp. 384-385)

4. Discuss how you might use your children's invented spelling in planning your word analysis instruction in the classroom. Provide a rationale for your ideas. (pp. 392-393)

Multiple Choice Questions

1. Research begun in the mid-60's which examined the effectiveness of various approaches to reading instruction found that: (pp. 375-376)
    a. phonics was more effective than "whole-word" instruction
    b. the best predictor of reading success was the ability to recognize the letters of the alphabet
    c. teaching effectiveness was more important than the type of instructional approach used
    d. both b and c above

2. Results of studies on the effectiveness of phonics instruction conclude that (p. 377)
    a. word analysis skills are essential for automaticity in reading
    b. phonics should be taught in a meaningful context
    c. word analysis is being taught differently today than it has been in the past
    d. all of the above

3. Young children who are able to memorize the lines to a poem displayed on a chart, but who cannot yet recognize any of the same words out of context, are probably in which stage of word-recognition ability? (p. 378-379)
    a. logographic
    b. transition from logographic to beginning alphabetic
    c. alphabetic
    d. orthographic

4. A child who focuses primarily on the individual letters in sounding out words and who reads in a slow laborious manner, is probably at which stage of word-recognition? (p. 378-379)
    a. logographic
    b. transition from logographic to beginning alphabetic
    c. alphabetic
    d. orthographic

5. An analytic approach to phonics instruction is better than a synthetic approach because: (p. 383)
    a. a synthetic approach emphasizes letter-sound relationships
    b. an analytic approach emphasizes letter-sound relationships
    c. an analytic approach begins with meaningful units
    d. both a and c above

6.	Children who occasionally write a "p" instead of a "q," are most likely demonstrating: (p. 387)
	a. their level of knowledge regarding letters and sounds
	b. a learning disability
	c. the need for further practice with the letter "p"
	d. both a and c above

7.	Phonemic segmentation is important because: (p. 390)
	a. it develops the ability to direct and focus attention on separate sounds in a word
	b. it usually develops before children enter school
	c. it can be developed largely through rhyming activities
	d. both a and b above

8.	Which stages of invented spelling require skills similar to those involved in phonemic awareness and phonemic segmentation? (p. 392)
	a. prephonemic and phonemic
	b. phonemic and letter-name
	c. letter-name and transitional
	d. transitional and derivational

9.	The best answer to the question, "What's the first thing you do when you come to a word you don't know?" is: (pp. 423; 221)
	a. read to the end of the sentence in which the word is found
	b. look at the parts of the word for meaning clues
	c. try to pronounce the word and check for meaning
	d. all of the above

10.	The purpose of teaching children rapid word recognition and word analysis is: (pp. 369,417)
	a. to help them develop automaticity in reading
	b. to enable children to have better comprehension when they read
	c. to help those children learn to read who have not had extensive experience with books prior to coming to school
	d. all of the above

Answers to Multiple Choice Items

1. d
2. d
3. a
4. c
5. c
6. a
7. a
8. b
9. a
10. d

Notes:

Chapter 9. Developing Children's Literacy Abilities in Content Areas

Chapter Summary

Chapter 9, "Developing Children's Literacy Abilities in Content Areas," explores ways to guide children's reading and writing in subject areas. Specific instructional strategies are emphasized including a combination of the content Directed Reading-Thinking Activity (Content DR-TA), Group Mapping Activity (GMA), and the Vocabulary Self-Collection Strategy (VSS). Additional strategies include the K-W-L Plus (Know-Want to Know-Learned), the Directed Inquiry Activity (DIA), writing workshop in subject area instruction, guiding beginning research, and project-based and theme cycle learning in content areas.

The central focus of this chapter is that children construct meaning as they read and write; content learning is thus increased as children pursue topics of interest and respond in writing to text. Writing here is viewed as more than simply a means for recording what is learned; rather, it is a means for extending the learning itself. Theme cycles, project-based learning, the Foxfire approach, and visual literacy projects are recommended as ways to bring reading, writing, and subject matter learning into an integrated whole. A final discussion in this chapter explores study skills as important, but not in themselves sufficient, components in content area learning.

Teaching Suggestions

1.   Have students work in partners or small groups to share their DEJ "Literacy History in Subject Area Learning" and their choice of instructional strategies that suit their style. Lead a discussion that explores issues brought up in the text discussion on pages 434-440 concerning differential reading abilities, the need for teacher guidance in reading all subject areas, and Nancie Atwell's poignant report-writing memory.

2.   Demonstrate the combination Content DR-TA, GMA, and VSS using a duplicated content passage. Give students the full 6-8 minutes for initial brainstorming of the general topic; note when/if the noise level reduces and then increases again. Observe the discussions, taking notes about what you see and snatches of conversation. Move all the way through the GMA and VSS, even if means doing so at a rapid pace, so that students can feel what it's like to be accomplished "old hands" at mapping and VSS. In the debriefing ask students to analyze the learning event they just experienced; add your observations:

> "I saw people <u>laughing</u> - you mean you can learn and laugh at the same time?"

> "In this group an expert emerged - and actually became the expert for the whole class. Isn't it nice that Annick speaks French?"

The Content DR-TA, GMA, and VSS combination is always fun to debrief because students see immediately that their familiarity with GMA and VSS makes them more powerful participants in the learning event. We are then able to make the point that the kind of learning we're stressing when we combine content and literacy instruction gets better as we go along; that is, after using VSS or any other strategy once it gets better when we use it the second, third, and fourth time. Prepare overhead transparencies for BLM 9-1, What Students Need to Do When Learning from Text, (text p. 441) and BLM 9-2, What Teachers Need to Do to Guide Students' Learning from Text, (text p. 442) and use in the debriefing. Walk through HOW TO DO (text pp. 447-448) and the BUILDING TABLE (text pp. 474-475).

3.   Prepare two copies of BLM 9-3, the K-W-L Plus Handout, for each student. Demonstrate the K-W-L Plus in much the same way as noted for the Content DR-TA, GMA, VSS combination (see above). In the debriefing note how similar these strategies are and how useful they are as alternatives. Walk through the HOW TO DO (text p. 451) and BUILDING TABLE (text pp. 474-475).

4.   Use the reading prompts on page 453 to demonstrate subject area Reading Response Groups or develop prompts for a passage of your choice. You may want to combine this with initial activities for a project-based or theme cycle unit (see Teaching Suggestions for Chapter 7). Debrief the process. Walk through the HOW TO DO (text p. 454) and BUILDING TABLE.

5.   Discuss and walk through the Beginning Research HOW TO DO (p. 463-464). You may wish to demonstrate parts of the activity; e.g., listening and notetaking and reading and notetaking. Emphasize how this sequence of events works to lead children away from the copy-the-encyclopedia approach we all used so well in the middle grades (and beyond). Note how this strategy might precede a project-based or theme cycle unit. Have students meet in small groups and brainstorm how they would actually use this strategy in a class.

6.   Assign lesson plans for one or more chapter instructional strategies.

Black Line Masters for Chapter 9

BLM 9-1 (text p. 441) What Students Need to Do When Learning from Text
BLM 9-2 (text p. 442) What Teachers Need to Do to Guide Students' Learning from Text
BLM 9-3 (not in text) K-W-L Plus Worksheet

Evaluation Options

1. Your observations of student participation in small and large group demonstrations and discussions.

2. Your evaluation of students' lesson plans (see #6 above).

3. Your evaluation of student responses to Short Answer Essay Questions (see items below). Please note that we have provided page numbers that are keyed to the text indicating where the content related to each question is located. You may wish to use these questions as a study guide for your students rather than as an evaluation option.

4. Your evaluation of Multiple Choice Questions (see items below). Again, you will find each questions is keyed to the text content and you may wish to use these questions as a study guide.

5. Your evaluation of students' portfolios.

Short Answer Questions

1. Contrast the " study skills" perspective of subject area learning with the "meaning construction" perspective presented in this chapter. (pp.431-432; 467-468)

2. In what ways is the K-W-L Plus strategy similar to the content directed DR-TA? In what ways are the two strategies different? (pp.443-444; 448-449)

3. Write three prompts you would use for a fifth grade reader response group studying a unit on the solar system. (p.452-455)

4.Choose a topic for a unit of study at a grade level of your choice. Discuss how you would go about teaching your students the process of gathering information and developing individual research projects based upon this topic. (pp. 459-461; 463-464)

Multiple Choice Questions

1. In planning for content area instruction, a teacher: (pp. 434; 440)
   a. must provide for transactions between the reader and the text
   b. have as a goal to create thoughtful readers and writers in subject areas
   c. keep content area reading and writing separate from language arts activities
   d. both a and b above

2. "Real learning" in the classroom is characterized by: (p. 440)
   a. students' engagement with their peers
   b. the ability to write one's thoughts coherently
   c. the ability to complete homework assignments with no further help
   d. all of the above

3. In guiding students' learning from text, teachers should: (p. 442)
   a. make sure they have all the details of their units planned out in advance
   b. make sure that students have tapped into their prior knowledge
   c. teach notetaking skills before students have read the material
   d. both a and b above

4. The advantage of using the DR-TA, GMA, and VSS in the content areas is that: (pp. 446-447)
   a. these strategies enable children to guide their own thinking
   b. these strategies allow children to actively engage in learning
   c. social interaction is an integral part of these strategies
   d. all of the above

5. Asking students to write down everything they have learned that day is a prompt used in : (pp 456-458)
   a. learning logs
   b. journals
   c. double entry journals
   d. both a and b above

6. The main difference between the prompts used to guide a literature response group and those used with content area reader response groups is that: (pp. 452-453)
   a. prompts for literature response groups are more wide-ranging
   b. prompts for content area response groups should not focus as much on the children's own experiences
   c. prompts for content area response groups should derive from ideas in the text
   d. both a and c above

7. Research on writing across the curriculum has shown that: (pp. 432-433)
    a. children must be taught how to write effectively in the content areas
    b. writing can help students gain further insights
    c. writing is used most effectively for displaying what one knows
    d. both a and b above

8. The main difference between learning logs and journals is that: (pp.456-458)
    a. children don't brainstorm in journals
    b. only in journals do children write what they have learned
    c. journals allow children to dialogue with their teacher through their writing
    d. both a and c above

9. Some teachers do not guide their students' reading of subject area texts because: (pp. 436)
    a. these teachers erroneously believe that children transfer their reading skills automatically to subject areas
    b. round robin reading has proven effective in covering the material
    c. only the children that are poor readers have difficulty with subject area texts
    d. both a and c above

10. Research projects like Foxfire, which are generated by the students themselves, represent a way of putting into practice: (pp. 465-467)
    a. theme cycles
    b. Piaget's theory
    c. visual literacy
    d. all of the above

Answers to Multiple Choice Items
1. d
2. a
3. b
4. d
5. d
6. d
7. d
8. c
9. a
10. d

Notes:

Chapter 10. Understanding Language, Cultural, and Achievement Diversity in the Classroom

Chapter Summary

Chapter 10, "Understanding Language, Cultural, and Achievement Diversity in the Classroom," focuses students' attention on the importance our attitudes toward children whose primary culture and language or dialect are different from the prevailing culture and language of school. The discussion then develops three types of classroom-based strategies and activities that have been effectively used in developing English language and literacy with bilingual students from diverse and different language and cultural backgrounds. The first consists of strategies designed to develop background and conceptual knowledge and include Sheltered English, the Vocabulary Self-Collection Strategy (VSS), and Vocabulary Journals.

The second set of strategies emphasize meaning construction and meaning monitoring and include the Directed Listening-Thinking Activity (DL-TA), the Directed Reading-Thinking Activity (DR-TA), Question-Answer Relationships (QAR), Reciprocal Questioning (ReQuest), and Reciprocal Teaching. And the third strategy group emphasizes motivation of individual and group responses to literature. These are the Read-Aloud Strategy, Literature Response Journals, Investigative Questioning Procedure (InQuest), and the use of Multicultural/Multiethnic Literature. A compilation of multicultural/multiethnic children's literature provides an important resource in this chapter.

This discussion also emphasizes the important role of the teacher in working with children who have special needs including physical diversity, developmental learning diversity, emotional diversity, and giftedness.

The chapter concludes with a discussion of four levels of multicultural education and ideas for creating a multicultural classroom environment.

Teaching Suggestions

1. Use the Double Entry Journal (DEJ), emphasizing prior student knowledge on diversity and student's revised understanding of diversity through mapping, in small and large group discussions.

2. This chapter can also be effectively introduced by focusing students' attention on the two transcripts featuring Lionel (p. 479) and the children using Hawaiian creole English (p. 480) at the beginning of the chapter. Encourage your students to explore the effect of teacher sensitivity and understanding of language and cultural diversity on children's self-esteem (particularly their self-esteem as a learner) and motivation for learning. Through small group or partner team discussion ask your students to examine how Krashen's "affective filter" (p. 484) and the instructional

requirements for optimal success (pp. 484-485) influence children's motivation to acquire a new language.

3.   Identify student volunteers to form a discussion panel, with you as moderator, on the topic "The Effect of Legislation on Ethnic and Gender Diversity in Classroom Instruction." The discussion on pp. 481-482 will serve as beginning background reading on this topic. Encourage your students to connect this discussion to current ethnic, immigration, and gender issues discussed in the media. The following questions can be used to initiate the panel discussion. What impact do you believe the legislation enacted over the past half-century has had on classroom instruction? What effect does it have on your teaching? Why do you believe the change process designed to meet instructional needs for children from diverse ethnic and language groups takes so long to implement in the classroom? Following the panel discussion summarize and synthesize the key ideas developed.

4.   As a class assignment arrange for your students to observe in an elementary classroom where nonmainstream English and/or bilingual children are represented. With the cooperation of the classroom teacher they should identify one child to observe during literacy instruction. Next, ask them to describe the child's dialect and/or proficiency in English (see discussion on pp. 490-500). Finally, briefly address the following questions: How does the child respond and communicate with the teacher? with other children? How does the teacher communicate with the child? with other children? How would you describe the child's attitude toward learning and classroom instruction? How would you describe the teacher's attitude toward the child and her or his progress? Their observations and responses should be developed in a two to three page written discussion. Your evaluative response to these observations will provide important insights into your students' understanding of key concepts developed in this chapter.

5.   Have students work in small groups to develop a sheltered English lesson from the principles and HOW TO DO instructions on pages 502-503 in the text. Provide each group with a narrative text and a content area text; emphasize the responsibility classroom teachers have both for bilingual students' English language development, including general literacy development, and for their learning in subject areas. As an assignment have students develop sheltered English lesson plans.

Evaluation Options

1. Your observations of student participation in small and large group discussions.

2. Your reading and evaluative response to the written assignment (see #4 above) and/or lesson planning (see #s 4 & 5 above).

3. Your evaluation of student responses to Short Answer Essay Questions (see items below). Please note that we have provided page numbers that are keyed to the text indicating where the content related to each question is located. You may wish to use these questions as a study guide for you students rather than as an evaluation option.

4. Your evaluation of Multiple Choice Questions (see items below). Again, you will find each question is keyed to the text content and you may wish to use these questions as a study guide.

5. Your evaluation of students' portfolios.

Short Answer Essay Questions

1. Choose one of the major legal decisions discussed in this chapter and describe how it may have affected your own experiences in school. (pp. 481-482)

2. On page 483 of your text, the authors discuss seven instructional principles in working with linguistically and culturally diverse children. Identify one instructional strategy form this chapter (or from previous chapters) and explain how these principles are incorporated in this strategy. (pp. 483)

3. Select one of your favorite children's books and discuss how you would prepare a lesson for reading the book aloud using a Sheltered English approach. (pp. 502-503)

4. Identify one instructional strategy discussed in this chapter that you would consider most effective for use with gifted students. Briefly explain the strategy and why you believe it will be highly effective with these students. (pp.523)

Multiple Choice Questions

1. Because of cultural differences children may vary in: (p. 483)
   a. their ability to pay attention in class
   b. their ideas about turn-taking when speaking
   c. their cognitive ability
   d. none of the above

2. According to Krashen's affective filter hypothesis, students learning English as a second language:(pp. 484-485)
   a. should have frequent practice in pronunciation
   b. learn better in a "low anxiety" environment
   c. often demonstrate poor affect
   d. both a and b above

3. A child learning English as a second language who achieves a score at the 90th percentile on the Comprehensive Test of Basic Skills is demonstrating: (pp. 486-487)
   a. CALP
   b. BICS
   c. facility with context-embedded language
   d. none of the above

4. According to recent research on language acquisition: (p. 485-487)
   a. children learn English mainly through social interaction with peers
   b. children learn vocabulary terms first, then begin to string words together to form sentences
   c. children are more concerned with communicating than with using the standard form
   d. all of the above

5. The main instructional goal for children who speak a non-mainstream dialect is: (pp.490-491)
   a. the acquisition of standard English forms before beginning literacy instruction
   b. the development of appropriate social interaction patterns
   c. the development of literacy
   d. both b and c above

6. A kindergarten classroom in which all the children speak Chinese, and the teacher speaks only English, would be most likely designated as: (p. 494-495)
   a. bilingual
   b. transitional
   c. a two-way bilingual program
   d. sheltered English

7. According to Gunderson's Elementary ESL Decision Heuristic (1991), a student whose English is characterized by simple sentences but who only occasionally initiates conversation and who has had 3 years of literacy instruction in his/her native language, would benefit from: (pp. 499-500)
   a. reading nursery rhymes in English
   b. review of the letter-sound relationships in English
   c. sheltered English in the content areas
   d. none of the above

8. Multicultural/multiethnic literature is useful for:
   a. mainstream students
   b. enabling minority students to experience an identification with the story characters
   c. exploring issues of racism
   d. all of the above

9. A child described as having dyslexia: (pp. 519-520)
   a. may benefit from work on phonemic awareness and phonemic segmentation
   b. probably sees letters backwards
   c. has a brain lesion
   d. none of the above

10. According to Banks (1993), which of the four approaches to multicultural teaching is illustrated in the following example: a social studies unit in which the pioneering roles of African Americans, Chinese Americans, Latinos, Native Americans and whites are studied in the settling of the "Old West": (pp. 527-528)
    a. the Contributions approach
    b. the Additive approach
    c. the Transformation approach
    d. The Social Action approach

Answers to Multiple Choice Items
1. b
2. b
3. a
4. c
5. c
6. d
7. c
8. d
9. a
10.c

Notes

Chapter 11. Evaluating Children's Progress in Reading and Writing

Chapter Summary

Chapter 11, "Evaluating Children's Progress in Reading and Writing," will help your students become proficient in using informal observations in their teaching. Special attention is given to the instructional use of information gathered from informal group discussions and classroom reading and writing experiences. The discussion develops the use of the informal reading inventory and miscue analysis and the use of portfolio evaluation. Recommendations are presented to assist your students in effective communication with parents regarding their children's progress.

Formal achievement testing, including values and limitations, is also discussed. The central focus of this discussion, however, is on the effective use of observations to provide information that can be used to plan and enhance the reading and literacy growth of children.

Teaching Suggestions

1. Use the Double Entry Journal (DEJ), on student memories of reading and writing assessment in school and the way in which these were and were not examples of authentic assessment, in small and large group discussions.

2. Ask your students examine Marlene's Story (p. 543, Figure 11-1) and to consider what observations they have that provides important clues to Marlene's literacy progress (see discussion pp. 542-544). As you develop this discussion encourage them to turn to pp. 123-124, Table 3-3, Early Reading and Writing Assessment Checklist, (recall BLM 3-2 from Chapter 3) and apply this checklist to Marlene's Story. Summarize the discussion by emphasizing the importance of informal observation as a key information source in instructional planning.

3. Prepare overhead transparencies and handouts of BLM 11-1 and BLM 11-2, the Developmental Inventory, (text pp. 747-548). Walk students through the inventory pointing out how various instructional strategies make it possible to observe specific literacy behaviors (e.g., predicting in DL-TAs, DR-TAs, and K-W-L Plus). Have students duplicate copies of the inventory and give them an assignment to use the inventory during the week observing one or more children. Emphasize that it is not intended that they "stop and observe;" rather, their observations should occur in the regular course of classroom events.

4. Present the In and Out-of-School Interest Inventory by making an overhead transparency for (BLM 11-3 (text p. 553). Encourage your students to consider the nature of the information collected in this inventory. (Note for

example that items #1-#5 relate to in-school reading, while items #6-#10 pertain to out-of-school activities and interests.) Discuss how this information would be used in developing insights into children's literacy interests and instructional planning. You can effectively connect this discussion to the transcript from Jenny Sirell's kindergarten class on "What makes a good reader?" found in Chapter 3 (pp. 88-90).

5. Develop the discussion on the Informal Reading Inventory, Miscue Analysis, and Recording Miscues (see pp. 563-569). Begin by using an overhead transparency of BLM 11-4, Recording Miscues, (text pp. 567-568) to discuss the recording system. To provide practice in using the miscue analysis system photocopy BLM 11-5, Unmarked Text for the Angela Passage, for each member of your class. Ask your students to complete miscue notations on this clear text page as you present the oral reading found at the bottom of page 568 (The Transcript). Make an overhead transparency of BLM 11-6, Marked Miscue Transcript for Angela Passage, (text p. 569) and present this to your students. Discuss and clarify the miscue notational system and encourage your students to place an interpretation on this brief example (see p. 569).

Now make a sufficient number of photocopies for each member of your class of BLM 11-7, the Unmarked page of text "A Trip to the Store". Encourage your students to complete miscue notations as you present a simulation of Rebecca's oral reading using "Rebecca's Miscue Transcript" (see p. 570). You will need to practice reading the transcript ("A Trip to the Store") a bit in order to present an accurate rendering. We also find it is helpful to present "Rebecca's reading" a second time in order for students to feel comfortable with the miscue notational system. After completing the miscue reading use an overhead transparency of BLM 11-8, Rebecca's Miscue Transcript, (text p. 570) and discuss the miscue notations. Next, present an overhead transparency of BLM 11-9. Rebecca's Comprehension Responses, (text pp. 570-571) and discuss these responses. Finally, explore the nature of Rebecca's oral reading miscues and her comprehension responses to develop an interpretation and implications for instruction (see pp. 571-575, "Interpreting Miscues").

Black Line Masters (BLM) for Chapter 11

BLM 11-1 (text p. 547) Developmental Inventory - Listening/Reading
BLM 11-2 (text p. 548) Developmental Inventory - Speaking/Writing
BLM 11-3 (text p. 553) In- and Out-of-School Inventory
BLM 11-4 (text pp. 567-568) Recording Miscues
BLM 11-5 (text p. 569) Unmarked Text for Angela Passage
BLM 11-6 (text p. 569) Marked Miscue Transcript for Angela Passage
BLM 11-7 (not in text) Unmarked page of text "A Trip to the Store"
BLM 11-8 (text p. 570) Rebecca's Miscue Transcript for "A Trip to the Store"

BLM 11-9 (text p. 570-571) Rebecca's Comprehension Responses

Evaluation Options

1) Your observations of student participation in small and large group discussions.

2) Your evaluation of student responses to Short Answer Essay Questions (see items below). Please note that we have provided page numbers that are keyed to the text indicating where the content related to each question is located. You may wish to use these questions as a study guide for you students rather than as an evaluation option.

3) Your evaluation of Multiple Choice Questions (see items below). Again, you will find each question is keyed to the text content and you may wish to use these questions as a study guide.

4) Your evaluation of students' portfolios

1. What is meant by authentic assessment? Why is it important for literacy instruction? (pp. 539-542)

2. Discuss how Ruddell's Developmental Inventory (1993) in Figures 11-2 and 11-3 on pages 547 and 548 addresses the seven principles of assessment presented at the beginning of this chapter. (pp. 546-551; 539-542)

3. Select a grade level that you are interested in teaching. Discuss what types of items you might include in your students' literacy portfolios and explain the criteria you would use for selecting these items and evaluating these portfolios. (pp. 552-563)

4. Suppose you are teaching in a second grade class. Briefly outline your plan for communicating a child's literacy progress to his/her parents. Discuss how you might modify this plan for children from homes where no English is spoken. (pp. 579-585)

Multiple Choice Questions

1. Authentic assessment: (pp. 539-542)
   a. involves observations of children
   b. uses samples of the children's reading and writing
   c. focuses on process, as well as product
   d. all of the above

2. Standardized reading tests: (pp. 540, 538)
   a. rarely assess the process of meaning construction
   b. take into account students' prior knowledge
   c. are used by school districts in making policy decisions
   d. both a and c

3. A student whose style when writing letters to friends differs from the style he/she uses in writing letters to a children's literature author is demonstrating progress in which area of Ruddell's Developmental Inventory (1993)? (pp. 547-550)
   a. guides audience through text
   b. knows how text works
   c. understands social aspects of meaning construction
   d. all of the above

4. The major difference between portfolio assessment and a simple compilation of students' work over the course of a grading period is: (pp.552-563)
   a. in portfolios, the selection of what to include is based on predetermined instructional objectives
   b. there are a fewer range and variety of samples in a portfolio
   c. portfolios include observations of students
   d. both a and c above

5. An eight year old girl has recently entered your third grade class. A sample of her oral reading was taken in order to complete a miscue analysis. Use the following excerpt to answer questions 5, 6, and 7:

   Text: The people are banking uptown.
   Child's reading: "The peoples be bakin' uptown."

   How many miscues are there in the child's reading? (pp.564-571)
   a. 4
   b. 3
   c. 2
   d. 1

6.　The child's reading shows evidence of: (pp.564-575)
　　　a. dialect differences
　　　b. meaning interference problems
　　　c. dyslexia
　　　d. both a and b above

7.　Saying the word "bakin'" for "banking" is an example of (pp. 567-569)
　　　a. substitution
　　　b. omission
　　　c. transposition
　　　d. none of the above

8.　If the report cards in your district only provide for grades of A, B, C, etc. in broad subject areas, you should: (p. 584)
　　　a. refuse to use them
　　　b. explain to parents how limiting the report cards are
　　　c. use your informal assessments to write additional comments
　　　d. b and c above

9.　The SAT college entrance exam in an example of: (pp.585-586)
　　　a. a survey test
　　　b. a norm-referenced test
　　　c. a test battery
　　　d. all of the above

10.　A fifth grade child who achieves a score at the 80th percentile rank on a reading achievement test: (pp. 588-589)
　　　a. can probably read at the 8th grade level
　　　b. has scored equal to or above 80% of the students in the original norm group
　　　c. got 80% of the test items correct
　　　d. both a and b above

Answers to Multiple Choice Items
1. d
2. d
3. d
4. d
5. d
6. d
7. a
8. c
9. d
10. b

Notes:

Chapter 12. Examining Instructional Approaches:
Basal Reader, Literature-Based, Whole Language and Supplementary Programs

Chapter Summary

In Chapter 12, "Examining Instructional Approaches - Basal Reader, Literature Based, Whole Language, and Supplementary Programs," your students will be introduced to the three most used approaches to reading and literacy instruction in the nation. This discussion develops the background and philosophy that underlie each of these approaches and shows how they work in the classroom. Chapter coverage includes discussion of lesson plans, student literature anthologies, workbooks, core literature selections, and the use of previously discussed strategies and activities such as language based stories, recording and sharing children's stories, oral story sharing, and writing workshop.

You will also find specific criteria identified to assist your students in the selection of supplementary reading and writing programs, computer software programs, and in the adoption of textbooks.

This chapter will be of particular value to your students as a resource for information about instructional approaches that allows them to (a) understand thoroughly and implement the approach for which they feel the most affinity, (b) work productively in a school or district that mandates a specific approach, and (c) combine aspects of one approach with another as they work to change their current teaching practice.

Teaching Suggestions

1. Use the Double Entry Journal (DEJ), on the "ideal reading and writing program" and where the program fits on the "instructional continuum of beliefs (p. 610)," in small and large group discussions.

2. Encourage your students to think about the changes that have occurred across the last century in reading and writing (language arts) instruction. Locate a reading or writing program (or grade level sample materials from several programs) published between 1910 and 1960 in your curriculum library. Also locate a program (or grade level sample materials from several programs) published within the last ten years. Divide your class into small groups and provide a program sample from the 1910-1960 period and a recent program sample. Ask each student group to briefly contrast these two text samples from the two time periods with particular attention to story content, story interest, cultural and gender diversity, and skill emphasis (place the 1910-1960 and 1980-1990s in two columns at the top of the chalkboard with the content analysis categories down the left side). Discuss the influences in a changing and technological oriented nation on the materials used and content, the instructional emphasis, and teacher

preparation (see pp. 600-601, Table 12.1) for the two time periods. Have each group briefly share findings. Make an overhead transparency from BLM 12-1, Historical Perspective on Reading and Literacy Instruction, (text pp. 600-601) to assist in the synthesize and summarization of key influences and ideas and incorporate the small group and class discussion.

3.   Encourage your students to examine the instructional continuum found on page 610 (Figure 12.6). Use small group or partner pair discussions to discuss the following questions: "Where would you place you own personal instructional belief system on this continuum? Why? What role does teacher decision-making play in determining the instructional emphasis on skill development and meaning construction in a given instructional approach (phonics, basal reader, literature-based, and whole language)?

4.   Have students work in small groups or partners to begin planning a year-long language, reading, and writing instructional program. They will need to identify the instructional approach and the materials they intend to use. As out-of-class work, they are to gather materials and resources for their program, develop a written plan specifying program rationale and components. If appropriate have students write lesson plans using instructional strategies learned in Chapters 3 through 10. If those chapters have not been covered, have students add lesson plans to their program as coverage allows.

5.   Develop the key ideas related to the evaluation and selection of instructional programs using an overhead transparency of BLM 12-5, Instructional Program Evaluation Checklist,(text p. 645) with your students. Also photocopy a sufficient number of copies of the Checklist for each member of your class. Emphasize that many of your students will at some time in their teaching careers be involved in the selection of textbooks for their school or school district. Carefully examine the Instructional Program Evaluation Checklist and the rating scale from "Poor" (1) to "Outstanding" (5). Bring in several sample texts from various grade levels for at least two reading (or language arts) programs. Be sure to include not only the children's texts but also the Teacher's Manuals, workbooks and other support materials. Have your students break into small groups and use the Evaluation Checklist to assist in examining samples from the instructional programs, identifying strengths and limitations. Have each group briefly summarize and report their findings and recommendations. (Note: A similar activity could be developed around the evaluation of computer software by using BLM 12-4, Developmental Scale for Rating Computer Software, (text p. 642).

6.   Ask each student to complete the following brief writing assignment related to an instructional approach of her or his choice. Each student will need to arrange for a classroom visit with a teacher who relies heavily on the selected approach (Basal, Literature-Based or Whole Language). Encourage

students (in partners or in small groups) to review our discussion on the specific approach selected (Basal Reader - pp. 610-622; Literature-Based - pp. 622-633; Whole Language - pp. 633-641). Ask them to design a brief checklist of instructional features and strategies that they expect to find during their observation. They should pay particular attention to the way in which reading and writing is integrated in the social context of the classroom for each approach. Following their observation of the selected approach encourage each student (or student partner pair) to find a few minutes to interview the teacher to explore her or his views on the advantages and limitations of this approach. Ask each student to provide a brief summary discussion (two to three pages) based on the checklist and her or his expectations. Provide an brief evaluative response to each student's observation.

Black Line Masters for Chapter 12

       BLM 12-1 (text pp. 600-601) Historical Perspective on Reading and Literacy Instruction, 2 pp.

       BLM 12-2 (text p. 610) An Instructional Continuum of Beliefs About Reading and Literacy Development

       BLM 12-3 (text p. 642) Developmental Scale for Rating Computer Software

       BLM 12-4 (text p. 645) Instructional Program Evaluation Checklist

Evaluation Options

1. Your observations of student participation in small and large group discussions.

2. Your reading and evaluative response to item #6 above.

3. Your evaluation of student responses to Short Answer Essay Questions (see items below). Please note that we have provided page numbers that are keyed to the text indicating where the content related to each question is located. You may wish to use these questions as a study guide for you students rather than as an evaluation option.

4. Your evaluation of Multiple Choice Questions (see items below). Again, you will find each question is keyed to the text content and you may wish to use these questions as a study guide.

5. Your evaluation of students' portfolios.

<u>Short Answer Questions</u>

1. Select one period from the four presented in Table 12-1 on pages 600-601. Discuss the relationship between key influences during that period and the literacy materials used, the instructional emphasis in reading and writing, and teacher preparation. (pp. 600-601)

2. Compare and contrast a basal reader approach with either a literature-based or whole language approach. (pp. 610-641)

3. Decide which of the 3 approaches, i.e. basal reader, literature-based, or whole language, most suits your own philosophy and capabilities as a teacher. Provide a brief rationale for your choice. (pp. 609-643)

4.Suppose you are asked to be on a committee to review the language arts textbooks for your district. Explain what type of textbook you would adopt based upon the criteria discussed on pages 644-646 of this chapter. (pp. 644-646)

Multiple Choice Questions

1. Materials with a moralistic emphasis were most likely to be found:(pp. 602-605)
    a. in the 1920's
    b. when the primary reason for literacy was the reading of the Bible
    c. in McGuffey's readers
    d. both b and c above

2. The placement of students into reading groups according to reading level (e.g. preprimer, primer, 1-1 etc.) was more widespread: (pp. 600-601; 634-640)
    a. before whole language was popular
    b. around World War I
    c. in the earliest years of our country
    d. none of the above

3. The widespread notion that there is a wide spread literacy crisis in this country:(p. 608)
    a. is not supported by the actual data on literacy achievement
    b. does not take into consideration historical figures on literacy rates
    c. provides evidence that teachers are not as well educated as in the past.
    d. both a and b above

4. Basal readers: (pp.610-622)
    a. may require less teacher preparation time
    b. contain more expository readings than narrative ones
    c. have predetermined skill strands
    d. both a and c above

5. The best way of using a basal series is: (pp. 621-622)
    a. not to deviate from the guidelines
    b. to supplement it with other materials and activities
    c. to use it only with poor readers
    d. none of the above

6. The key difference between the literature-based approach and the basal approach is: (pp. 610-633)
    a. Basals encourage teachers to group readers by ability
    b. Basals don't include good children's literature selections
    c. Literature-based approaches require more planning and expertise on the part of a teacher
    d. both a and c above

7. A literature-based approach: (pp. 622-633)
   a. precludes the teaching of phonics
   b. uses core sets of trade books for literacy instruction
   c. is more expensive than any other approach
   d. both b and c above

8. The main difference between a literature-based approach and a whole language approach is(are): (pp. 633-641)
   a. whole language emphasizes the integration of reading, writing, and subject area learning
   b. literature-based approaches use full-length works of children's literature
   c. these approaches use different strategies for developing comprehension
   d. both a and c above

9. Which of the following reading approaches is best? (pp. 644-646)
   a. whole language
   b. literature-based
   c. basal
   d. an approach which is meaning-centered

10. In evaluating instructional materials, one should consider: (pp. 644-645)
    a. the "user friendliness" of the teacher's guide
    b. the extent to which diversity is represented in story selections
    c. how well the program can be adapted to a variety of different instructional philosophies
    d. all of the above

Answers to Multiple Choice Items
1. d
2. a
3. d
4. d
5. b
6. d
7. b
8. a
9. d
10.d

Notes:

Chapter 13. Organizing and Managing Classrooms for Literacy Learning

Chapter Summary

Chapter 13, "Organizing and Managing Classrooms for Literacy Learning," presents classroom organization and management recommendations for early and beginning readers and for each of the three major literacy instructional approaches (basal reader, literature-based, and whole language). The chapter emphasizes that classroom organization and management in guiding children's reading and writing development involve far more than discipline; further, the chapter asserts that what teachers believe about how children learn has a powerful influence on organization and management issues - e.g., physical arrangement of the room, materials and equipment in the room, orchestration of classroom schedules and events, time allocation and use, and establishment of classroom rules and routines.

Each section of the chapter addressing early reading and writing, basal reading, literature-based, and whole language instruction begins with underlying beliefs and assumptions about that type of learning and teaching; following are suggestions and models for physical organization of the classroom, organization of the classroom day, and management issues for each.

Teaching Suggestions

1.   Have students in small groups or partners share the results of the Content DR-TA DEJ responses they made. Have them focus on the areas they wish to "work on a bit."

2.   Prepare overhead transparencies for BLM 13-1, 13-4. 13-8, and 13-11, the Underlying Beliefs and Assumptions About Literacy Learning for early readers and the three instructional approaches (text pp. 660, 671, 678-679, & 686) and BLM 13-2, 13-3, 13-5, 13-9, and 13-11, Organization of the Classroom Day charts for K-1 and the three instructional approaches (text pp. 666, 667, 674, 682, & 689). Have students work in small groups; assign each group a level (i.e., K-1) or an instructional approach (basal, literature-based, whole language). Using the text as a beginning point each group is to design a classroom, develop the schedule for the classroom day, and address management issues they believe important. Groups are to be prepared to demonstrate how their plans follow from the beliefs and assumptions for the type of instruction they are addressing. If you have sufficient board space have each group draw their classroom and write their daily schedule on the board. In discussing each plan, use the overhead transparencies to support the ensuing discussion.

3.   Prepare an overhead transparency and handouts for BLM 13-12, the Project Work Management Sheet (text p. 691). Lead a discussion about how this

sheet may be used to guide students' and groups' work each day. Refer back to activities you did previously involving independent group work (see Teaching Suggestions Chapters 7 and 9).

Black Line Masters for Chapter 13

> BLM 13-1 (text p. 660) Underlying Beliefs and Assumptions About Literacy Learning: Early and Beginning Readers and Writers
> BLM 13-2 (text p. 666) Organization of the Kindergarten Day: Half Day
> BLM 13-3 (text p. 667) Organization of the Kindergarten Day: Whole Day
> BLM 13-4 (text p. 671) Underlying Beliefs and Assumptions About Literacy Learning: Basal Reading Instruction
> BLM 13-5 (text p. 674) Organization of the Classroom Day - Basal Reader Instruction
> BLM 13-6 (text p. 675) Scheduling Basal Reading Groups - Week 1
> BLM 13-7 (text p. 676) Scheduling Basal Reading Groups - Weeks 2 and 3
> BLM 13-8 (text pp. 678-679) Underlying Beliefs and Assumptions About Literacy Learning: Literature-Based Instruction
> BLM 13-9 (text p. 682) Organization of the Language Arts Period - Literature-Based Instruction
> BLM 13-10 (text p. 686) Underlying Beliefs and Assumptions About Literacy Learning: Whole Language Instruction
> BLM 13-11 (text p. 689) Organization of the Classroom Day - Whole Language Instruction
> BLM 13-12 (text p. 691) Project Work Management Sheet

Evaluation Options

1.   Your observations of student participation in small and large group demonstrations and discussions.

2.   Your evaluation of students' organizational plans.

3.   Your evaluation of student responses to Short Answer Essay Questions (see items below). Please note that we have provided page numbers that are keyed to the text indicating where the content related to each question is located. You may wish to use these questions as a study guide for your students rather than as an evaluation option.

4.   Your evaluation of Multiple Choice Questions (see items below). Again, you will find each questions is keyed to the text content and you may wish to use these questions as a study guide.

5.   Your evaluation of students' portfolios.

Short Answer Questions

1. List what you remember about the organization and management of classrooms when you were in elementary school. What beliefs and assumptions about literacy learning and what instructional approaches might have been behind these practices? (pp. 654-656)

2. Select a grade level of your choice and make a map of how you would organize your classroom. Provide a rationale for your plan based upon your personal philosophy about literacy instruction and the instructional approach you hope to use. (pp. 670-693)

3. How are the assumptions about early literacy learning listed on page 660 of your text addressed by the establishment of play centers in a kindergarten classroom? (pp. 660, 664-665)

4. Discuss the advantages and disadvantages of ability grouping. What role will ability grouping have in your classroom and how is this role consistent with your personal philosophy? (pp. 677-678)

Multiple Choice Questions

1. Discipline problems usually arise: (p. 659; 669)
   a. when classroom management fails
   b. when the teacher is a novice
   c. when the teacher is not organized
   d. both a and c above

2. A kindergarten play area might include: (pp. 664-665)
   a. social studies materials
   b. paper and writing tools
   c. a puppet theater
   d. all of the above

3. A play area is important for the development of literacy in a kindergarten classroom because: (pp. 660, 664-665)
   a. it provides for rich language interaction
   b. children can pretend to engage in authentic reading and writing activities (e.g. writing receipts in a play "store")
   c. it allows children to develop patterns of social interaction
   d. all of the above

4. Which of the following approaches is exemplified by small group, teacher-led reading instruction during a set time period each day? (pp. 671-674)
   a. basal
   b. whole language
   c. literature-based
   d. either a or b above

5. Basal readers should not be stored in children's desks because: (p. 673)
   a. during round robin reading, you want to hear the children's first attempt at reading the selection
   b. they can be better preserved by storing them in a central location
   c. activities such as the DR-TA would be less effective if the children had access to the stories before they were discussed during instruction.
   d. both b and c above

6. The main difference between the use of small groups in a basal approach and using small groups in a literature-based approach is that: (pp. 671-674; 678-686)
   a. children choose the selections they want to read in a literature-based approach
   b. children are ability grouped in a basal approach
   c. these groups are more likely to be child-directed in a literature-based approach
   d. all of the above

7.   An advantage of a literature-based program is that: (pp. 682-685)
     a. children stay with the same group throughout the year
     b. the materials have high interest to children
     c. it is easy to determine if group discussions are focused on the
        material
     d. both b and c above

8.   One of the major points to remember about establishing a whole language
     classroom is that:(pp. 690-692)
     a. because the tasks children are doing demand high involvement few
        discipline problems will arise
     b. the teacher must have a way of bringing order and consistency into
        the environment
     c. children must learn to evaluate their own behavior and resolve
        problems that occur
     d. both b and c above

9.   The notion that children must be provided with opportunities for
     exploration and self-directed inquiry is part of: (pp. 692-693)
     a. a whole language approach
     b. the basal reading approach
     c. the approach used by the majority of teachers in schools today
     d. none of the above

10. Which of the following has the greatest effect on how teachers manage their
     classroom? (pp. 653-656)
     a. how much experience they have
     b. how many ESL children are in the classroom
     c. their own beliefs about how children learn
     d. the number of students in the class

1. d
2. d
3. d
4. a
5. d
6. d
7. b
8. d
9. a
10.c

Notes:

Chapter 14. Continuing Professional Change and Growth: Reaching the Influential Teacher Goal

Chapter Summary

In Chapter 14, "Continuing Professional Change and Growth: Reaching the Influential Teacher Goal," your students are encouraged to remain open to new ideas that will continue to enhance their teaching effectiveness in reading and literacy development. This discussion explains the process of personal change and growth and encourages each student to reflect on his or her own teaching philosophy and belief system. The importance of developing a personal support system through contact with professional organizations, influential peer teachers, the principal, and supportive parents is stressed.

We also encourage each student to continue her or his professional growth and connections through in-service and staff development, professional conferences, and continuing education. Finally, this chapter is designed to assist each of your students in identifying his or her areas of greatest strength as well as need emphasis areas that will lead to the professional goal of becoming an influential teacher - a teacher who will have a significant influence on the personal and academic lives of children.

Teaching Suggestions

1. Use the Double Entry Journal (DEJ), on "important areas of professional change and growth" and "resources available for immediate and long range action," in small and large group discussions.

2. Develop the discussion around "The Change Process and Teacher Characteristics" (see pp. 702-707). Develop an overhead transparency from BLM 14-1, Teacher Styles, Characteristics, and the Change Process (text p. 705) and use it to discuss the four teacher styles and related characteristics with particular focus on the change process (New Ideas/Change Potential). Use partner pairs or small groups and encourage each student to examine the four teacher styles and characteristics in relation to self. Ask students to speculate on what influences in their lives (parents? influential teachers? peers?) may have shaped their beliefs about change. Involve the total class in a discussion of the change process to identify key insights. Again, use BLM 14-1 to summarize ideas and insights from the student discussions.

3. After discussion of the text section on "Finding Support Through School Connections" (pp. 707-714 of text) ask students to brainstorm ideas that they believe will be of value to them during their first year (or this year) of teaching. List key ideas on the chalkboard and ask each students to identify and make notes on those that are most important to him or her. If you are working with student teachers ask each to arrange for an interview with an elementary teacher at the grade level of highest interest and

explore the topic of "How to Establish School Connections." The class summary notes should be used to create a series of questions for the interview. Encourage them to include such areas as influential peer teachers, the principal, and supportive parents. A brief summary of the interview identifying new ideas for developing school connections should be completed. You may wish to provide an evaluative response to the summary or provide time for partner pair shared discussions at the next class session.

4.   Provide information for your students on one or more of the following professional organizations (see pp. 717-719 in the text): a) the local reading council monthly meetings in your area; b) the annual State Reading Association Conference or the International Reading Association annual convention; c) the State English Teachers Conference or the National Council of Teachers of English Annual Convention; or d) a Whole Language Umbrella Conference. Encourage your students to become members of one or more of these professional organizations by providing student membership applications at the discounted student rate. You may wish to call the numbers listed in our discussion for student membership forms (note that two of these are toll-free 800 numbers). Finally, encourage your students to attend a professional organization meeting and select program presentations that are of high interest to them and to share new conference teaching ideas with a class partner.

5.   Encourage your students to reflect on their perception of self as an influential teacher. Use BLM 14-3, Self-Reflection and Introspection Teaching Checklist, (text p. 721) as an overhead transparency to facilitate this discussion. Also make photocopies of BLM 14-3 for each member of your class. Ask each student to use the checklist to identify her or his self-perceived instructional strengths and areas of emphasis that she or he wishes to strengthen. Request that each student develop a brief written response (two to three pages) identifying three specific personal goals and a plan (pp. 720-722 of text) to increase her or his teaching effectiveness in becoming an Influential Teacher. Provide an evaluative response to the goals and plan discussion.

Black Line Masters for Chapter 14
      BLM 14-1 (text p. 705) Teacher Styles, Characteristics, and the Change
            Process
      BLM 14-2 (text p. 714) Parent Volunteer Checklist Information
      BLM 14-3 (text p. 721) Self-Reflection and Introspection Teaching Checklist

Evaluation Options

1.   Your observations of student participation in small and large group discussions.

2. Your reading and evaluative response to suggestions #3 and #5 above.

3. Your evaluation of student responses to Short Answer Essay Questions (see items below). Please note that we have provided page numbers that are keyed to the text indicating where the content related to each question is located. You may wish to use these questions as a study guide for you students rather than as an evaluation option.

4. Your evaluation of Multiple Choice Questions (see items below). Again, you will find each question is keyed to the text content and you may wish to use these questions as a study guide.

5. Your evaluation of students' portfolios.

Short Answer Questions

1. Outline the 3-step process for change presented at the beginning of this chapter. Discuss a personal situation either at school or at work that illustrates this process. (pp.700-702)

2. The outline in Table 14-1 on page 705 indicates that the Nonsupportive-Productive teacher has low potential for accepting new ideas and change. Explain why this teacher style has low change potential using the ideas about the change process discussed on page 702 and 703. (pp. 702-706)

3. Suppose you were going to try to encourage a teacher to change from a basal approach to a literature-based approach. Describe what strategies you might use to do so, following the principles outlined on pages 702 and 703 and taking into consideration the teacher characteristics listed on pages 703-706. (pp. 702-706)

4. Identify three influential teacher or instructional areas in which you would like to continue your professional growth and develop a brief plan for implementing this growth. (pp. 720-722)

Multiple Choice Questions

1. According to Ruddell and Ruddell, the reason that so many new teachers leave the profession probably has to do with: (pp. 701-702)
    a. the low salaries
    b. they failed to understand the dynamics of change
    c. the number of students in the classroom
    d. poor support from the administration

2. The main reason that teachers who believe children learn skills in sequence may not be able to change to a whole language approach is that: (pp. 702-703)
    a. there is no advantage for doing so
    b. their knowledge and beliefs are incompatible with a whole language approach
    c. whole language is too complex for them to understand
    d. they will have no opportunity to observe a teacher using whole language

3. Inservice workshops may fail to produce changes in the way teachers carry out instruction because: (pp. 702-703; 716)
    a. these workshops are usually conducted during off-duty hours
    b. there is little opportunity for follow-up
    c. they cost too much money
    d. both b and c

4. A teacher who does not share in control of lessons with her students, who demonstrates little intellectual curiosity, but who says he/she wants to change: (pp. 703-707)
    a. has a low change potential
    b. has a moderate change potential
    c. has a high change potential
    d. is an anomaly

5. In order for a non-supportive, non-productive teacher to change, the following is required: (pp. 703-707)
    a. they must be mandated to do so by their principal
    b. they must be given a monetary incentive
    c. they must have plenty of opportunities to see their peers using the new ideas
    d. it's highly unlikely that they will change no matter what is done

6. Which of the following ideas from your reservoir of educational experiences should you rely on in your teaching? (pp. 707-708)
    a. former influential teachers' attitudes regarding student potential
    b. attitudes and instructional strategies of former ineffective teachers
    c. ideas you learned from your own experiences
    d. all of the above

7. Your inability to locate an influential peer teacher in your school, suggests that: (pp.709-710)
    a. you are teaching in a low SES area
    b. your peers did not graduate from the same teacher education program as you
    c. your peers are all much older than you
    d. you need to make more of an effort to get to know your peers

8. Arranging for the principal to visit in your classroom can: (pp. 710-711)
    a. enable you to get to know his/her beliefs and philosophy about education
    b. lessen your anxiety when she/he comes in to evaluate you
    c. motivate your children by providing them with an audience for their performances
    d. all of the above

9. How can parent volunteers improve your understanding of the children in your classroom? (pp. 711-714)
    a. you can observe parents interacting with their own children in the classroom
    b. you can observe the parents communicate with their children
    c. you can better understand parents' view of home literacy development
    d. all of the above

10. Membership in professional organizations is important because: (pp. 717-720)
    a. school districts require it
    b. it establishes a network of peers interested in similar ideas
    c. you can update your knowledge of the field
    d. both b and c above

Answers to Multiple Choice Items
1. b
2. b
3. b
4. a
5. c
6. d
7. d
8. d
9. d
10.d

Notes:

SHARED BELIEFS OF INFLUENTIAL TEACHERS ABOUT TEACHING

1. Personal Characteristics:
— energy, commitment, passion
— warmth and caring
— flexibility
— high expectations of self

2. Understand Learner Potential:
— sensitive to individual needs, motivations, and aptitudes
— understands "where students are"
— high demands on learners

3. Attitude Toward Subject:
— enthusiasm
— goal to create intellectual excitement
— consider alternative point of view

4. Life Adjustment:
— concern with student as a person
— attentive to academic problems and personal problems

5. Quality of Instruction:
— makes material personally relevant
— stresses basic communication: clear writing, comprehension of text material, critical thinking
— teaching is logical and strategy oriented:
  (a) clear statement of problem
  (b) use of familiar concrete examples
  (c) extension to more abstract examples
  (d) analysis of abstract concepts involved
  (e) application of concepts to new contexts
— goal to identify issues that should be considered before conclusions are reached
— need to engage students in the process of intellectual discovery

TABLE 1-2

IDENTIFYING MY PERSONAL BELIEF SYSTEM: TEACHING READING AND WRITING SKILLS

	Agree			**Disagree**	
1. Teaching reading is, for the most part, helping students understand the relationship between letters and sounds.	1	2	3	4	5
2. Using home and life experiences of the student is very important in helping students comprehend text.	1	2	3	4	5
3. It is important to make reading material personally relevant to each student.	1	2	3	4	5
4. Reading and writing are two very different skills and should not be taught in conjunction with each other.	1	2	3	4	5
5. High achievement expectation is important if students are to achieve at the optimal level.	1	2	3	4	5
6. Monitoring and feedback on student reading and writing responses is important for student success.	1	2	3	4	5
7. Students who speak a second language will have more difficulty learning to read than those who speak only English.	1	2	3	4	5
8. Nonverbal responses of students deserve little consideration in small group discussion.	1	2	3	4	5
9. Reading motivation can best be developed by providing clear signals indicating what response the teacher wants.	1	2	3	4	5
10. Clear, definite teaching goals and plans are critical for good reading and writing instruction.	1	2	3	4	5
11. Student comprehension can be greatly enhanced by engaging students in the process of intellectual discovery.	1	2	3	4	5
12. Exhibiting a positive attitude toward reading and writing or skills being taught is the mark of a good teacher.	1	2	3	4	5

SIX KEY COMPONENTS OF EXPERT READER COMPETENCIES

This brief introspective reading experience demonstrates how expert readers use six key components in the reading process:

1. Expert readers use print-to-meaning word analysis knowledge, consisting of letter-sound and letter-pattern–sound-pattern relationships, as well as visual meaning markers, to assist in constructing meaning. This process is for the most part automatic.

2. Expert readers possess language knowledge that enables them to infer meaning from relational and lexical elements within and across sentences.

3. Expert readers possess a literacy background and prior story knowledge that they draw upon to identify a story schema, such as folktale, which is helpful in inferring word and story meaning basic to understanding the story and story outcome.

4. Expert readers possess reading motivation, both internal and external, supporting their persistence and continued reading in the process of making meaning.

5. Expert readers' processing of text is interactive and involves meaning making using word, sentence, and story structure. This enables them to reach meaning closure and arrive at a conclusion about the story.

6. Expert readers are effective in drawing on comprehension strategies that enable them to use different levels of thinking (from simple recall to high-level inference) and monitor meaning construction in light of background knowledge, reading objective, and expected outcome.

CLASSROOM LANGUAGE

FUNCTION	ORAL FORM	WRITTEN FORM
Informal Personal Exchange	Greetings	Personal notes to friends
	(Interactional, Personal)	
	Communications of feelings	Unedited written experiences
	(Instrumental, Interactional, Personal)	
	Control of others' behavior	Memos and directions
	(Instrumental, Regulatory)	
Formal Information Exchange	Classroom discussion	Edited experience stories
	(Informational, Heuristic)	
	Classroom lectures	Edited reports
	(Informational)	
	Public talks	School textbooks
	(Informational)	
Literary Exchange	Drama and theater	Poetry, narrative, drama
	(Imaginative, Informational, Heuristic)	

—— TABLE 2-1

Classroom Language Functions (Halliday's language functions are noted in parentheses)

BLM 2-3 (text p. 60) The Meaning Construction Process - Meaning Negotiation Between Teacher and Child

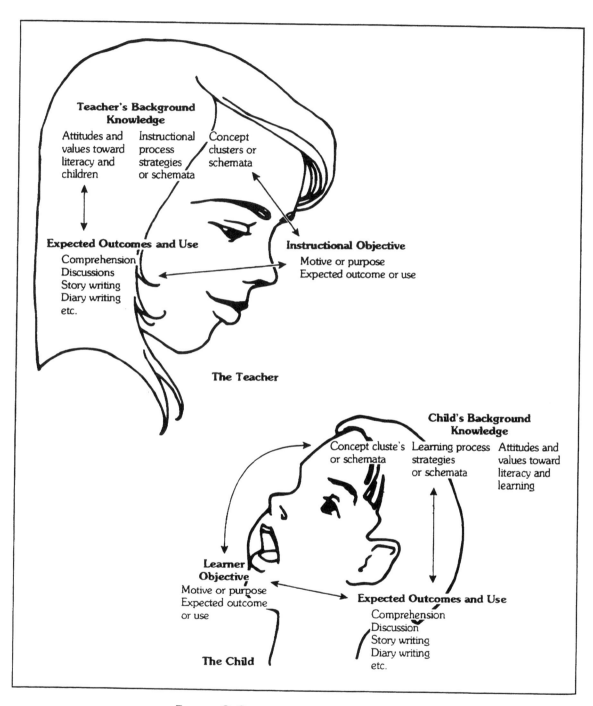

FIGURE 2-3

The Meaning Construction Process—Meaning Negotiation Between Teacher and Child

BLM 3-1 (text p. 76) Meaning Negotiation in Classroom Interaction Using Personal, Group, Text, and Task Meanings

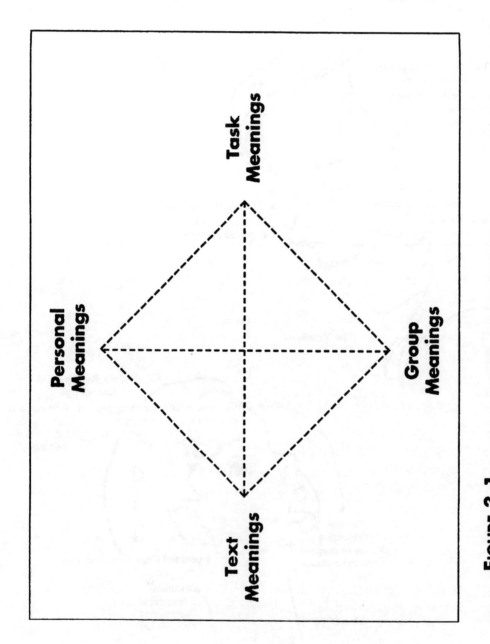

FIGURE 3-1

Meaning Negotiation in Classroom Interaction Using Personal, Group, Text and Task Meanings. (Reproduced with permission from Harris, 1989, p. 143.)

Student Name _____ **Grade** _____

Dates Observed _____

Instructions: Circle the appropriate letter to assess your student's progress.
R = Rarely; O = Occasionally; U = Usually

A. Understands Language of Instruction and Group Participation

1. Knows direction words, ordering words, color words, feeling- and sensory-based words _____ R O U

2. Can follow instructional directions _____ R O U

3. Can participate and cooperate in group activities and is tolerant of other children's viewpoints _____ R O U

4. Understands how to ask questions to clarify a task meaning or text meaning problem _____ R O U

5. Understands how to ask questions to clarify a personal or group problem_____ R O U

B. Understands Picture- and Print- Awareness Knowledge

6. Knows that pictures and print represent ideas and meaning _____ R O U

7. Understands that pictures used in sequence can tell a story _____ R O U

8. Knows concept of letter, word, sentence, and role of special punctuation marks _____ R O U

9. Knows that print is read in left-to-right direction, that lines are read from top-to-bottom, and that pages have top and bottom positions and are organized from left-to-right _____ R O U

10. Understands that pictures and print can be used to tell a story and explain ideas _____ R O U

C. Knows How to Use Observing, Recording, and Writing Knowledge

11. Understands that thoughts and ideas can be recorded through drawing and writing _____ R O U

12. Writes fluently to produce stories and descriptions _____ R O U

13. Can use written conventions such as story titles and capital letters _____ R O U

14. Understands specific vocabulary that reflects order and sequence of events _____ R O U

15. Can use ideas to create or recreate experiences based on classroom and field trip experiences _____ R O U

D. Demonstrates Sense of Story and Narrative

16. Understands that a story has characters, settings, events, and plot _____ R O U

17. Can follow and understand events in story sequence _____ R O U

18. Can develop inferences and predictions about story events and outcomes and support these using story content or background knowledge _____ R O U

19. Can comprehend and retell a story to other children or the teacher _____ R O U

20. Can and does read—conventionally or otherwise _____ R O U

E. Demonstrates Positive Attitude Toward Reading and Literacy Activities

21. Enjoys story reading and story-sharing time _____ R O U

22. Shows enthusiasm toward exploring picture and storybooks _____ R O U

23. Likes to share personal stories and books with a friend or small group _____ R O U

24. Enjoys small group discussion of ideas related to books which have been shared or read during story sharing _____ R O U

25. Enjoys creating new stories based on a shared story _____ R O U

Special observation notes:

This checklist may be used without permission.

TABLE 3-3

Early Reading and Writing Assessment Checklist

DEVELOPING A LESSON PLAN

STEP ONE: Identify the lesson focus (e.g., comprehension, vocabulary) or topic (subject area). For this class you will also need to identify the grade level.

STEP TWO: Identify and <u>write out</u> the lesson objectives. To do this, ask yourself, **"What do I want students to know or be able to do when this lesson is finished?".** Make a list.

STEP THREE: List all materials and equipment needed (don't forget things like extension cords, file cards, pocket charts, etc.).

    1.   List all materials and equipment <u>you</u> are to supply for the lesson.

    2.   List all materials and equipment <u>students</u> are to bring or are expected to have available.

    3.   Note any materials or equipment you need to prepare or assemble.

STEP FOUR: Think about and decide how your lesson will accomplish the following goals:

    1.   Build on students' <u>prior knowledge base</u>. How will you link what children are reading or writing to what they already know? How will you allow students to examine what they already know in light of the new information you are presenting or preparing them to read?

    2.   **Guide students' reading of text** and exploration of new ideas. How will you guide students before, during, and after reading? How will you prepare them for new concepts, new vocabulary, and new ideas? How will you develop their ability to be increasingly accomplished readers?

    3.   Promote <u>in-depth understanding</u>. How can students get beyond the surface to explore, examine, and manipulate ideas and things? What are you doing to promote active comprehension of text and higher-level thinking?

    4.   Provide for <u>integration</u> of new information into students' current knowledge base. How will you design instruction so that students analyze and synthesize information, see relationships, and formulate new ideas?

    5.   **Guide students' written and/or oral response to texts** and lessons. How will you assist students in anchoring new concepts,

vocabulary, and knowledge? How will you guide them in linking new information to their prior knowledge base? How will they elaborate and expand ideas? How will you prepare them to become increasingly articulate?

STEP FIVE: Write out explicitly all instructional procedures for the lesson.   Your procedures should include all of the following:

1.   An **Introduction** in which you

   - gain and focus student attention

   - introduce and identify the lesson focus or topic

   - engage student's interest

   - **prepare students for reading**

   HINT: Really good lesson introductions generally involve more student-talk than teacher-talk. Avoid talking a lot to start a lesson.

2.   A **Sequentially Developed Plan** for moving from start to finish of the lesson. This plan should state

   - what you will do during each part of the lesson

   - what questions you will ask and what directions you will give

   - **how you will guide and develop students' reading and writing during the lesson**

   - estimations of time allowances for various activities

3.   A **Conclusion** that brings closure and signals the lesson's end. Your conclusion should

   - recapitulate and review what occurred in the lesson

   - include homework or other assignments for extending the lesson

   - provide feedback to let students know how they did

   - indicate how you will evaluate or grade assignments made

STEP SIX: Reflect on and evaluate the lesson

1.   What did you like best about the lesson?

2.   What didn't you like?

3.   What activities and events generated student interest and participation?

4.   What activities and events went awry or got out of control?

5.   **<u>How well did the lesson guide and develop students' reading and writing?</u>**

6.   What adjustments would improve the lesson?

143

SAMPLE LESSON PLAN FORMAT

Class_____ Date _____

Lesson Focus or Topic_____Grade Level _____

Lesson Objectives:

1._____

2._____

3._____

4._____

5._____

Materials/Equipment Needed:

1._____   2_____

3._____   4_____

5._____   6_____

Instructional Procedures (with time approximations):

Introduction_____

_____

_____

_____Time _____

Sequence of Events and Instructions to be given or Questions asked_____

_____

_____

_____

_____

_____

_____

_____Time _____

Conclusion_____

_____

_____Time _____

Lesson Evaluation:

What went right_____

_____

_____

_____

What didn't go right_____

_____

_____

Adjustments that would improve the lesson_____

_____

_____

_____

BLM 4-1 (text p. 141) Levels of Thinking

	LEVELS OF THINKING			
	FACTUAL	INTERPRETIVE	APPLICATIVE	TRANSACTIVE
COMPREHENSION SKILLS				
1. Identifying Details	X	X		
2. Sequence of Events	X	X		
3. Cause and Effect	X	X	X	X
4. Main idea	X	X	X	X
5. Predicting Outcomes	X	X	X	X
6. Valuing	X	X	X	X
7. Problem Solving	X	X	X	X

TABLE 4-1

An Instructional Framework for Comprehension Development

146

A child asks, "Which one is Willy?"

T: Can't you tell? (*Focusing, factual level, identifying details*)

C1: No.

T: I don't know. It's hard to tell. How could you tell them apart? (*Focusing, interpretive level, identifying details*)

C1: Because he's a wind-up mouse.

T: Anything else about them that was different? (*Extending, interpretive level, identifying details*)

C2: Yes, he had a key.

T: Yes, anything else? (*Extending, interpretive level, identifying details*)

C3: Round—wheels.

T: Yes, maybe.

C4: Kind of like an egg.

T: Sort of.

C4: His ears were like two drops of tears.

T: Well, that's a good description. Can you think of anything else about the way Mr. Lionni chose to make the mice? (Wait time, 5 seconds) Here's Alexander. Here's Willy (shows picture of each). (*Extending, interpretive level, cause and effect*)

C3: One's rounder.

C2: One of them is smooth, and the other one's rough.

T: Why do you suppose one's smooth and one's rough? (*Raising, applicative level, cause and effect*)

C3: Because one's a toy.

T: Which one would that be, the smooth one or the rough one? (*Clarifying, interpretive level, cause and effect*)

C2: The smooth one.

T: That's probably the one I would choose—because I would think of a toy — (interrupted).

C4: Because a real mouse would have fur.

T: And so he wouldn't be very smooth would he? (*Extending, interpretive level, cause and effect*)

C3: No, he would be rough with hair sticking out.

This teacher is in the process of concluding the story discussion, also using *Alexander and the Wind-Up Mouse.*

T: What did you like about the story? (*Focusing, factual or interpretive level, identifying details*)

C1: I liked the part where he found the pebble.

T: You like where he found the pebble. Where did he find it, Timmy? (*Extending, factual level, identifying details*)

C1: By a box.

T: Where? (*Extending, factual level, identifying details*)

C1: By a box.

T: By a box. What were some of the things that were in the box? (*Extending, factual level, identifying details*)

C2: Dolls—(interrupted).

T: There were old toys in that box. Why had they been placed there? (*Extending, factual level, cause and effect*)

C3: Because they were old and couldn't work.

T: And they couldn't work. What did they plan to do with them, Henry? Henry, what did they plan to do with old toys? (*Extending, factual level, sequence of events*)

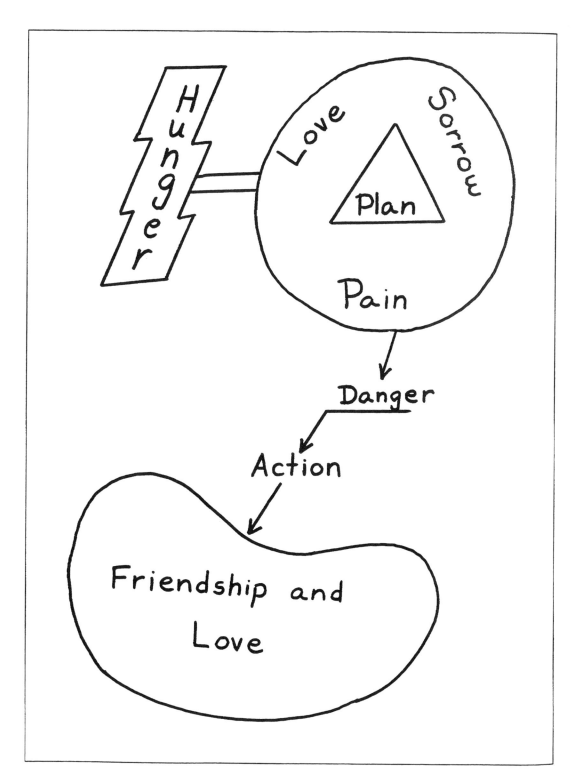

FIGURE 4-3 A

Sample Maps for Introducing the Group Mapping Activity. (Reproduced with permission from Ruddell Haggard, 1986, pp. 5 and 6.)

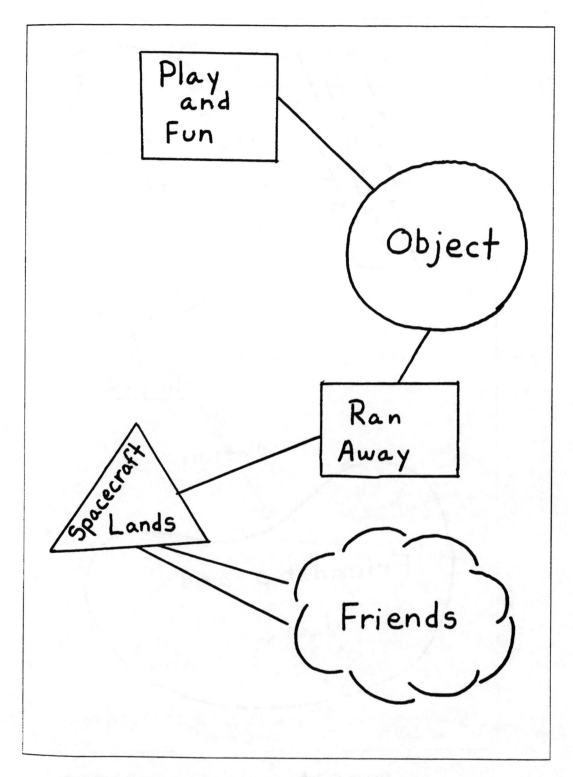

FIGURE 4-3 B

Sample Maps for Introducing the Group Mapping Activity. (Reproduced with permission from Ruddell Haggard, 1986, pp. 5 and 6.)

 Map the Story

The Bears on Hemlock Mountain

In the space below, draw a STORY MAP to show what you think this story is about. You may use lines, circles, squares, or any other shapes to make your Story Map.
REMEMBER: a map is not a picture. It is your way of showing what happens in the story.

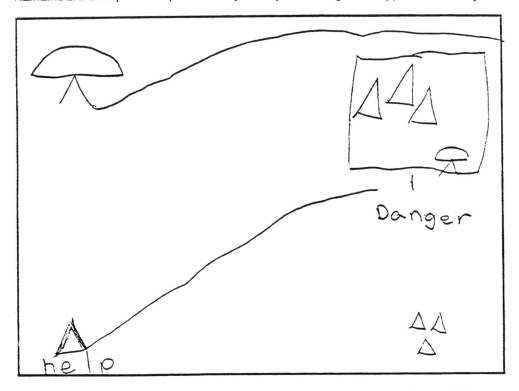

Now, share your Story Map with a friend and tell why you chose to draw what you did.

Shared with _Carey_ .

FIGURE 4-4.

Carey's Sample Map Using the GMA Strategy

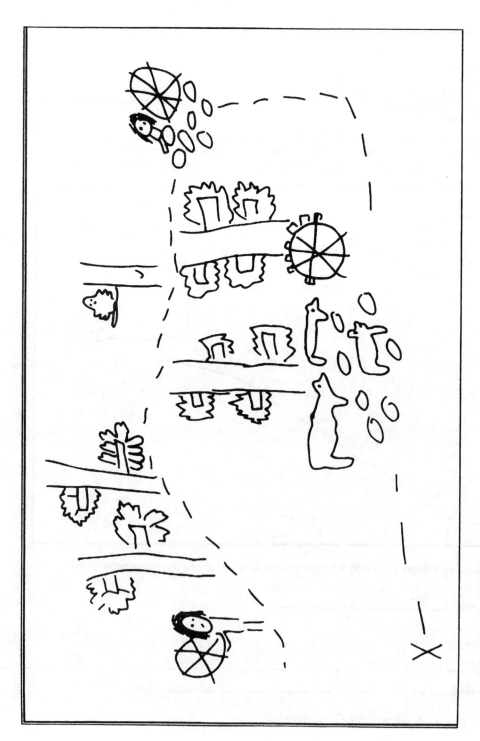

FIGURE 4-5

Alita's Map of *The Bears on Hemlock Mountain*

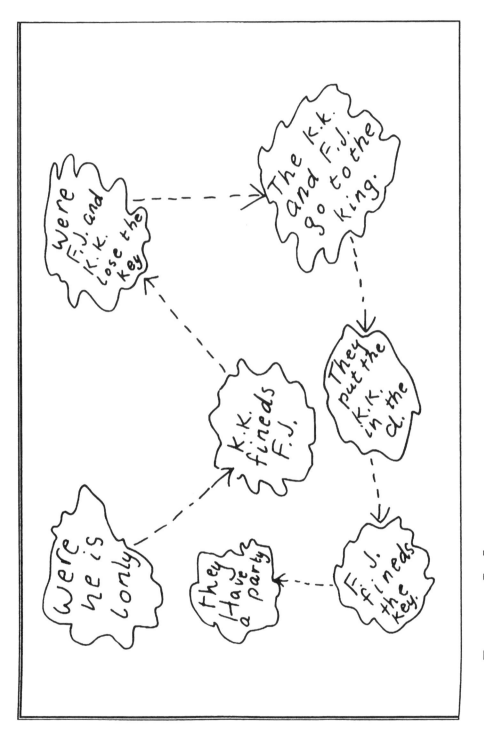

FIGURE 4-6

Alita's Map of Flibbity Jibbet and the Key Keeper

WHEN YOU COME TO A WORD YOU DO NOT KNOW, CHECK

1. **CONTEXT—read to the end of the sentence in which the word is found.** Are there meaning clues in the sentence? Are there meaning clues in other parts of the paragraph or story to this point? Using these clues do you think you know what the word means? Does it make sense? If so, go right on reading.

If Not

2. **STRUCTURE—look at parts of the word for meaning clues.** Do you recognize any roots or prefixes you know? Do any of the endings help? Combine this information with the context clues. Does it make sense? If so, go right on reading.

If Not

3. **SOUND—try to pronounce the word and check for meaning.** Often we may not recognize the meaning of a word in print but when we hear it we know the meaning. Do you know this word? Use this information with the context of the sentence. Does it make sense? If so, go right on reading.

If Not

4. **REFERENCE—check a reference.** Are there any margin notes to help explain the meaning? Does the glossary in the text define the word? Look it up in a dictionary. Ask someone. Combine that information with information from context. Does it make sense? Go right on reading.

	4-legged	swims	learns tricks	cute	Found in wild
kitten					
goldfish					
dog					
bird					
snake					
rat					

FIGURE 5-7

Semantic Feature Analysis for "Pets"

	Features										
Words											

BLM 6-1 (text p. 274) Teachers' Favorite Books for Classroom Reading Center

Grade Level	Book Titles
Kindergarten	*Alligators All Around: An Alphabet* (Sendak); *Bringing the Rain to Kapiti Plain: A Nandi Tale* (Verna); *Cinderella* (Perrault); *Mother Goose: A Treasury of Best-Loved Rhymes* (Piper); *Peter and the North Wind* (Littledale); *The Very Hungry Caterpillar* (Carle); *Why Mosquitoes Buzz in People's Ears* (Aardema).
Grade 1	*Anansi the Spider: A Tale from the Ashanti* (McDermott); *Frog and Toad* (Lobel); *Little Bear* (Minarik); *Mr. Rabbit and the Lovely Present* (Zolotow); *Rosie's Walk* (Hutchins); *The Three Little Pigs* (Galdone); *The Very Busy Spider* (Carle).
Grade 2	*The House on East 88th Street* (Waber); *Miss Nelson Is Missing!* (Allard); *Miss Rumphius* (Cooney); *Owl Moon* (Yolen); *The Story of Ferdinand* (Leaf); *A Taste of Blackberries* (Smith); *Where the Wild Things Are* (Sendak).
Grade 3	*Charlie and the Chocolate Factory* (Dahl); *The Case of the Elevator Duck* (Berends); *The Hundred Dresses* (Estes); *Mufaro's Beautiful Daughters* (Steptoe); *Ramona Quimby, Age 8* (Cleary); *The Story of Jumping Mouse* (Steptoe); *Superfudge* (Blume).
Grade 4	*Bridge to Terabithia* (Patterson); *Dear Mr. Henshaw* (Cleary); *In the Year of the Boar and Jackie Robinson* (Lord); *Island of the Blue Dolphins* (O'Dell); *Mrs. Frisby and the Rats of NIMH* (O'Brien); *Sarah, Plain and Tall* (MacLachlan); *The Velveteen Rabbit* (Williams).
Grade 5	*The Dark Is Rising* (Cooper); *The Indian in the Cupboard* (Banks); *Johnny Tremain* (Forbes); *My Side of the Mountain* (George); *Robin Hood—Prince of Outlaws* (Miles); *The White Mountains* (Christopher); *Witch of Blackbird Pond* (Speare).
Grade 6	*Are You There, God? It's Me, Margaret* (Blume); *Hatchet* (Paulsen); *James and the Giant Peach* (Dahl); *The Lion, the Witch, and the Wardrobe* (Lewis); *Mrs. Frisby and the Rats of NIMH* (O'Brien); *The Secret Garden* (Burnett); *Where the Red Fern Grows* (Rawls).

—— **TABLE 6-2** ——

Teachers' Favorite Books for the Classroom Reading Center

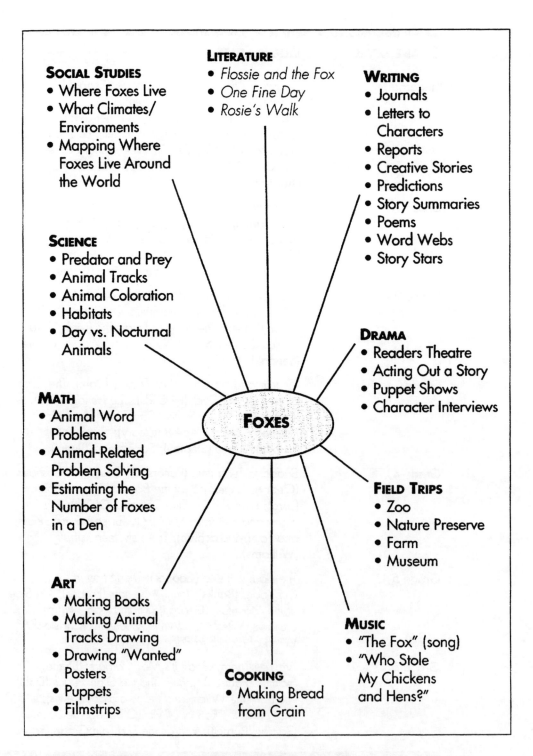

SOCIAL STUDIES
- Where Foxes Live
- What Climates/ Environments
- Mapping Where Foxes Live Around the World

SCIENCE
- Predator and Prey
- Animal Tracks
- Animal Coloration
- Habitats
- Day vs. Nocturnal Animals

MATH
- Animal Word Problems
- Animal-Related Problem Solving
- Estimating the Number of Foxes in a Den

ART
- Making Books
- Making Animal Tracks Drawing
- Drawing "Wanted" Posters
- Puppets
- Filmstrips

LITERATURE
- *Flossie and the Fox*
- *One Fine Day*
- *Rosie's Walk*

FOXES

WRITING
- Journals
- Letters to Characters
- Reports
- Creative Stories
- Predictions
- Story Summaries
- Poems
- Word Webs
- Story Stars

DRAMA
- Readers Theatre
- Acting Out a Story
- Puppet Shows
- Character Interviews

FIELD TRIPS
- Zoo
- Nature Preserve
- Farm
- Museum

MUSIC
- "The Fox" (song)
- "Who Stole My Chickens and Hens?"

COOKING
- Making Bread from Grain

— **FIGURE 6-1** —

Second-Grade Topical Thematic Literature Unit on Foxes

The Newbery Medal Award Books

John Newbery was the first English publisher of children's books. He lived from 1713 to 1767. The Newbery Medal Award, given in his honor, is one of the most prestigious awards in children's literature. It is given each year by the Association for Library Service to Children (American Library Association) to the author of the most distinguished children's literature published in the United States. The Newbery Medal Books given since the first award in 1922 are identified below. Quickly skim this list and place a check beside of those books that you read as a child. Which of the new titles would you like to read?

1922 The Story of Mankind by Hendrik Willem van Loon, Liveright.
1923 The Voyages of Doctor Dolittle by Hugh Lofting, Lippincott.
1924 The Dark Frigate by Charles Hawes, Atlantic/Little Brown.
1925 Tales from Silver Lands by Charles Finger, Doubleday.
1926 Shen of the Sea by Arthur Bowie Christman, Dutton.
1927 Smokey, The Cowhorse by Will James, Scribner.
1928 Gayneck, The Story of a Piegeon by Dhan Gopal Mukerji, Dutton.
1929 The Trumpeter of Krakow by Eric P. Kelly, Macmillan.
1930 Hitty, Her First Hundred Years by Rachel Field, Macmillan.

1931 The Cat Who Went to Heaven by Elizabeth Coatsworth, Macmillan.
1932 Waterless Mountain by Laura Adams Armer, Longmans.
1933 Young Fu of the Upper Yangtze by Elizabeth Foreman Lewis, Winston.
1934 Invincible Louisa by Cornelia Meigs, Little.
1935 Dobry by Monica Shannon, Viking.
1936 Caddie Woodlawn by Carol Brink, Macmillan.
1937 Roller Skates by Ruth Sawyer, Viking.
1938 The White Stag by Kata Seredy, Viking.
1939 Thimble Summer by Elizabeth Enright, Rinehart.
1940 Daniel Boone by James Daugherty, Viking.

1941 Call It Courage by Armstrong Sperry, Macmillan.
1942 The Matchlock Gun by Walter D. Edmonds, Dodd.
1943 Adam of the Road by Elizabeth Janet Gray, Viking.
1944 Johnny Tremain by Esther Forbes, Houghton.
1944 Rabbit Hill by Robert Lawson, Viking.
1946 Strawberry Girl by Lois Lenski, Lippincott.
1947 Miss Hickory by Carolyn Sherwin Bailey, Viking.
1948 The Twenty-one Balloons by William Pene du Bois, Viking.
1949 King of the Wind by Marguerite Henry, Rand.
1950 The Door in the Wall by Marguerite de Angeli, Doubleday.

1951 Amos Fortune, Free Man by Elizabeth Yates, Dotton/orig. publ., Aladdin.

1952 Secret of the Andes by Ann Nolan Clark, Viking.

1954 ... and now Miguel by Joseph Krumgold, Crowell.

1955 The Wheel on the School by Meindert DeJong, Harper.

1956 Carry on, Mr. Bowditch by Jean lee Latham, Houghton.

1957 Miracles on Maple Hill by Virginia Sorensen, Harcourt.

1958 Rifles for Watie by Hrold Keith, Crowell.

1959 The Witch of Blackbird Pond by Elizabeth George Speare, Houghton.

1960 Onion John by Joseph Krumgold, Crowell.

1961 Island of the Blue Dolphins by Scott O'Dell, Houghton.

1962 The Bronze Bow by Elizabeth George Speare, Houghton.

1963 A Wrinkle in Time by Madeleine L'Engle, Farrar.

1964 It's Like This, Cat by Emily Cheney Neville, Harper.

1965 Shadow of a Bull by Maia Wojciechowska, Atheneum.

1966 I, Juan de Pareja by Elizabeth Borten de Trevino, Farrar.

1967 Up a Road Slowly by Irene Hunt, Follett.

1968 From the Mixed-Up Files of Mrs. Basil E. Frankweiler by E.L. Konigsburg, Atheneum.

1969 The High King by Lloyd Alexander, Holt.

1970 Sounder by William H. Armstrong, Harper.

1971 Summer of the Swans by Betsy Byars, Viking.

1972 Mrs. Frisby and the Rats of NIMH by Robert C. O'Brien, Atheneum.

1973 Julie of the Wolves by Jean George, Harper.

1974 The Slave Dancer by Paula Fox, Bradbury.

1975 M. C. Higgins, the Great by Virginia Hamilton, Macmillan.

1976 The Grey King by Susan Cooper, Atheneum.

1977 Roll of Thunder, Hear My Cry by Mildred D. Taylor, Dial.

1978 Bridge to Terabithia by Katherine Paterson, Crowell.

1979 The Westing Game by Ellen Raskin, Dutton.

1980 A Gathering of Days: A New England Girl's Journey, 1830-32 by Joan W. Blos, Scribner.

1981 Jacob Have I Loved by Katherine Paterson, Crowell.

1982 A Vist to William Blake's Inn: Poems for Innocent and Experienced Travelers by Nancy Willard, Harcourt.

1983 Dicy's Song by Cynthia Voigt, Atheneum.

1984 Dear Mr. Henshaw by Beverly Cleary, Morrow.

1985 The Hero and the Crown by Robin McKinley, Greenwillow.

1986 Sarah, Plain and Tall by Patricia MacLachlan, Harper.

1987 The Whipping Boy by Sid Fleischman, Greenwillow.

1988 Lincoln: A Photobiography by Russell Freedman, Clarion.
1989 Joyful Noise: Poems for Two Voices by Paul Fleischman, Harper.
1990 Number the Stars by Lois Lowry, Houghton.

1991 Maniac Magee by Jerry Spinelli, Little Brown.
1992 Shiloh by Phyllis Reyonolds Naylor, Antheneum.
1993 Missing May by Cynthia Rylant, Orchard Books.

The Caldcott Medal Award Books

The Caldecott Medal, awarded by the Association for Library Service to Children (American Library Association), is named in honor of the well-known English illustrator Randolph Caldecott who lived from 1846 to 1886. This medal is awarded to the illustrator of the most distinguished picture book published in the United States each year. The Caldecott Medal Books (and honor books) have been selected since 1938. Review this list and check those books that you read as a child or, more recently, as an adult. Identify also those books that you think you would like to read and enjoy.

1938 <u>Animals of the Bible</u> by Helen Dean fish, ill. by Dorothy P. Lathrop, Lippincott.

1939 <u>Mei Li</u> wirtten and ill. by Thomas Handforth, Doubleday.

1940 <u>Abraham Lincoln</u> written and ill. by Ingrid and Edgar Parin d'Aulaire, Doubleday.

1941 <u>They Were Strong and Good</u> written and ill. by Robert Lawson, Viking.

1942 <u>Make Way for Ducklings</u> written and ill. by Robert McCloskey, Viking.

1943 <u>The Little House</u> written and ill. by Virginia Lee Burton, Houghton.

1944 <u>Many Moons</u> by James Thurber, ill. by Louis Slobodkin, Harcourt.

1945 <u>Prayer for a Child</u> by Rachel Field, ill. by Elizabeth Orton Jones, Macmillan.

1946 <u>The Rooster Crows</u> (traditional Mother Goose)ill. by Maud and Miska Petersham, Macmillan.

1947 <u>The Little Island</u> by Golden MacDonald, ill. by Leonard Weisgard, Doubleday.

1948 <u>White Snow, Bright Snow</u> by Alvin Tresselt, ill. by Roger Duboisin, Lothrop.

1949 <u>The Big Snow</u> written and ill. by Berta and Elmer Hader, Macmillan.

1950 <u>Song of the Swallows</u> written and ill. by Leo Politi, Scribner.

1951 <u>The Egg Tree</u> written and ill. by Katherine Milhous, Scribner.

1952 <u>Finders Keepers</u> by William Lipkind, ill. by Nicolas Mordvinoff, Harcourt.

1953 <u>The Biggest Bear</u> written and ill. by Lynd Ward, Houghton.

1954 <u>Madeline's Rescue</u> written and ill. by Ludwig Bemelmans, Viking.

1955 <u>Cinderella, or the Little Glass Slipper</u> by Charles Perrault, tr. and ill. by Marcia Brown, Scribner.

1956 <u>Frog Went A-Courtin</u> retold by John Langstaff, ill. by Feodor Rojankovsky.

1957 <u>A Tree is Nice</u> by Janice May Udry, ill. by Marc Simont, Harper.

1958 <u>Time of Wonder</u> written and ill. by Robert McCloskey, Viking.

1959 <u>Chanticleer and the Fox</u> adapted and ill. by Barbara Cooney, T. Crowell.

1960 <u>Nine Days to Christmas</u> by Marie Hall Ets and Aurora Labastida, ill. by Marie Hall Ets, Viking.

1961 <u>Baboushka and the Three Kings</u> by Ruth Robbins, ill. by Nicolas Sidjakov, Parnassus.

1962 <u>Once a Mouse</u> written and ill. by Marcia Brown, Scribner.

1963 <u>The Snowy Day</u> written and ill. by Ezra Jack Keats, Viking.

1964 <u>Where the Wild Things Are</u> written and ill. by Maurice Sendak, Harper.

1965 <u>May I Bring a Friend?</u> by Beatrice Schenk de Regniers, ill. by Beni Montresor, Atheneum.

1966 <u>Always Room for One More</u> by Sorche Nic Leodhas, ill. by Nonny Hogrogian, Holt.

1967 <u>Sam, Bangs & Moonshine</u> written and Ill. by Evaline Ness, Holt.

1968 <u>Drummer Hoff</u> by Barbara Emberley, ill. by Ed Emberley, Prentice.

1969 <u>The Fool of the World and the Flying Ship</u> by Arthur Ransome, ill. by Uri Shulevitz, Farrar.

1970 <u>Sylvester and the Magic Pebble</u> written and ill. by William Steig, Windmill Books.

1971 <u>A Story - A Story</u> written and ill. by Gail E. Haley, Atheneum.

1972 <u>One Fine Day</u> written and ill. by Nonny Hogrogian, Macmillan.

1973 <u>The Funny Little Woman</u> retold by Arlene Mosel, ill. by Blair Lent, Dutton.

1974 <u>Duffy and the Devil</u> by Harve Zemach, ill. by Margot Zemach, Farrar.

1975 <u>Arrow to the Sun</u> adapted and ill. by Gerald McDermott, Viking.

1976 <u>Why Mosquitoes Buzz in People's Ears</u> retold by Verna Aardema, ill. by Leo and Diane Dillon, Dial.

1977 <u>Ashanti to Aulu: African Traditions</u> by Margaret Musgrove, ill. by Leo and Diane Dillon, Dial.

1978 <u>Noah's Ark</u>, ill. by Peter Spier, Doubleday.

1979 <u>The Girl Who Loved Wild Horses</u> written and ill. by Paul Goble, Bradbury.

1980 <u>Ox-Cart Man</u> by Donald Hall, ill. by Barbara Cooney, Viking.

1981 <u>Fables</u> written and ill. by Arnold Lobel, Harper.

1982 <u>Jumanji</u> written and ill. by Chris Van Allsburg, Houghton.

1983 <u>Shadow</u> by Blaise Cendrard, trans. and ill. by Marcia Brown, Scribner.

1984 <u>The Glorious Flight: Across the Channel with Louis Bleriot</u> written and ill. by Alice and Martin Provensen, Viking.

1985 <u>St. George and the Dragon</u> retold by Margaret Hodges, ill. by Trina Schart Hyman, Little Brown.

1986 <u>The Polar Express</u> written and ill. by Chris Van Allsburg, Houghton.

1987 <u>Hey, Al!</u> by Arthur Yorinks, ill. by Richard Egielski, Farrar.

1988 <u>Owl Moon</u> by Jane Yolen, ill. by John Schoenherr, Philomel.

1989 <u>Song and Dance Man</u> by Karen Ackerman, ill. by Stephen Gammel, Knopf.

1990 <u>Lon Po Po: A Red Riding Hood Story from China</u> adapted and ill. by Ed. Young, Philomel.

1991 <u>Black and White</u> written and ill. by David Macaulay, Houghton.

1992 <u>Tuesday</u> written and ill. by David Wiesner, Clarion.

1993 <u>Mirrette on the High Wire</u> written and ill. by Emily Arnold McCully, Putnam.

Kids' Favorite Books: Children's Choices

These books are selected by about two thousand children in five test sites across the United States. Each year approximately five hundred new children's books are sent to each of the test sites for children's evaluation. The list has been produced from an ongoing joint project of the Children's Book Council and the International Reading Association for the last twenty years. This list for the year 1991 (the most recent list available) highlights the most popular books as viewed from the perspective of children (The Children's Book Council, Inc., and the International Reading Association, (1992). Kids' Favorite Books: Children's Choices 1989-1991. Newark, DE: International Reading Association.) The list is organized alphabetically and by suggested use level, ranging from "All Ages" through specific age levels. Take a few minutes and skim this list to identify those that you know and those you would like to become familiar with. What factors do you believe influence children's reading interests at various age levels based on this list?

All Ages

Beauty and the Beast by Marie Lerince de Beaumont, Simon and
    Schuster.
Black and White by David Macaulay, Houghton Mifflin.
The Empty Pot by Demi, Holt.
I Know an Old Lady Who Swallowed A Fly by Glen Rounds, Holiday House.
If You're Not Here Please Raise Your Hand: Poems about School by G. Brian
    Karas, Four Winds.
Oh, the Places You'll Go! by Dr. Seuss, Random House.
Seasons by Alberto Manguel, Doubleday.
The Tunnel by Anthony Browne, Knopf.

Beginning Independent Reading

Fish Eyes: A Book You Can Count On by Lois Ehlert, Harcourt Brace
    Jovanovich.
The Guy Who Was Five Minutes Late by Judy Glasser, HarperCollins.
Harry's Bath by Harriet Ziefert, Bantam.
Hi Bears, By Bears by Niki Yektai, Orchard.
A Hundred Million Reasons for Owning an Elephant (Or at Least a Dozen I Can
    Think of Right Now) by Lois G. Grambling, Barron's.
In the Haunted House by Eve Bunting, Clarion.
Lost! by David McPhail, Joy Street.
The Mixed-Up Mice Clean House by Robert Kraus, Warner.
My Mom Made Me Go to Camp by Judy Delton, Delacorte.

<u>My Perfect Neighborhood</u> by Leah Komaiko, HarperCollins.
<u>Never Spit on Your Shoes</u> by Denys Cazet, Orchard.
<u>One Cow Moo Moo!</u> by David Bennett, Holt.
<u>The Silly Book</u> by Babette Cole, Doubleday.
<u>Some Bodies in the Attic: A Spooky Pop-Up Book</u> by Keith Moseley, Grosset.
<u>"Stand Back," Said the Elephant, "I'm Going to Sneeze!"</u> by Patricia Thomas, Lothrop.
<u>Uncle Wizzmo's New Used Car</u> by Rodney A. Greenblat, HarperCollins.
<u>Who Goes Out on Halloween?</u> by Sue Alexander, Bantam.
<u>Who is the Beast?</u> by Keith Baker, Harcourt.
<u>The Winter Duckling</u> by Keith Polette, Milliken.

Younger Readers (5 to 8 years of age)

<u>Alice and the Birthday Giant</u> by John F. Green, Scholastic.
<u>Anna Marie's Blanket</u> by Joanne Barkan, Barron's.
<u>Blow Me a Kiss, Miss Lilly</u> by Nancy White Carlstrom, HarperCollins.
<u>Bye Bye Baby</u> by Janet Ahlberg and Allan Ahlberg, Little.
<u>Charlie Anderson</u> by Barbara Abercrombie, McElderry.
<u>The Completed Hickory Dickory Dock</u> by Jim Aylesworth, Macmillan.
<u>Cupid</u> by Babette Cole, Putnam.
<u>Daniel's Dog</u> by Jo Ellen Bogart, Scholastic.
<u>Dinosaur Garden</u> by Liza Donnelly, Scholastic.
<u>Eagle-Eye Ernie Comes to Town</u> by Susan Pearson, Simon & Schuster.
<u>Earrings!</u> by Judith Viorst, Atheneum.
<u>Herbie Hamster, Where Are You?</u> by Terence Blacker, Random House.
<u>Hey! Get Off Our Train</u> by John Burningham, Crown.
<u>The Hungry Thing Returns</u> by Jan Slepian and Ann Seidler, Scholastic.
<u>Little Grunt and the Big Egg: A Prehistoric Fairy Tale</u> by Tomie dePaola, Holiday House.
<u>Little Rabbit Foo Foo</u> by Michael Rosen, Simon & Schuster.
<u>Look Out, Patrick!</u> by Paul Geraghty, Macmillan.
<u>Mama Went Walking</u> by Christine Berry, Holt.
<u>Merry Christmas, Bigelow Bear</u> by Dennis Kyte, Doubleday.
<u>Miss Eva and the Red Balloon</u> by Karen M. Glennon, Simon & Schuster.
<u>Oh My Baby Bear!</u> by Audrey Wood, Harcourt Brace Jovanovich.
<u>Pondlarker</u> by Fred Gwynne, Simon & Schuster.
<u>Stay, Fang</u> by Barbara Shook Hazen, Atheneum.
<u>The Wedding of Brown Bear and White Bear</u> by Martine Beck, Little Brown.
<u>Well, I Never!</u> by Susan Pearson, Simon & Schuster.
<u>What If the Shark Wears Tennis Shoes?</u> by Winifred Morris, Atheneum.
<u>World Famous Muriel and the Magic Mystery</u> by Sue Alexander, Crowell.
<u>You Are Much Too Small</u> by Betty D. Boegehold, Bantam.

Middle Grades (8 to 10 years of age)

Ace: The Very Important Pig by Dick King-Smith, Crown.
The Adventures of Ratman by Ellen Weiss and Mel Friedman, Random House.
Amazing Lizards by Trevor Smith, Knopf.
Animal Camouflage: A Closer Look by Joyce Powzyk, Bradbury.
Animals in Danger: A Pop-Up Book by Wayne Ford, Aladdin.
The Bathwater Gang by Meredith Johnson, Little.
Brutus the Wonder Poodle by Linda Gondosch, Random House.
Buzz Beamer's Radical Sports by Bill Hinds, Little.
Choosing Sides by Hene Cooper, Morrow.
The Christmas Coat by Clyde Robert Bulla, Knopf.
The Cocker Spaniel by William R. Sanford and Carl R. Green, Crestwood House.
Fresh Brats by X.J. Kennedy, McElderry.
Fudge-a-Mania by Judy Blume, Dutton.
The Great Yellowstone Fire by Carole G. Vogel and Kathryn A. Goldner, Sierra
    Club/Little.
Handel and the Famous Sword Swallower of Halle by Bryna Stevens,
    Philomel.
Haunted Houses by Lewann Sotnak, Crestwood House.
The High Rise Glorious Skittle Skat Roarious Sky Pie Angel Food Cake by Nancy
    Willard, Harcourt.
Jack Galaxy, Space Cop by Robert Kraus, Bantam.
Jessie's Wishes by Sally Wittman, Scholastic.
Meg Macintosh and the Mystery at Camp Creepy by Lucinda Landon, Joy St.
Merry-Go-Round A Book about Nouns, Ruth Heller, Grosset.
Monsters of the Sea by Rita G. Gelman, Joy St.
Ms. Wiz Spells Trouble by Terence Blacker, Barron's.
Muggie Maggie by Beverly Cleary, Morrow.
On the Road with New Kids on the Block by Nancy E. Krulik, Scholastic.
Orp and the Chop Suey Burgers by Suzy Kline, Putnam.
Peace Begins with You by Katherine Scholes, Sierra Club/Little.
Play by Play: A Book of Games and Puzzles by Fred Winkowski, Little Brown.
Slime Time by Jim O'Conner and Jane O'Conner, Random House.
A Telling of the Tales: Five Stories by William J. Brooke, HarperCollins.
Twenty Ways to Lose Your Best Friend by Marilyn Singer, HarperCollins.
Vampires Don't Wear Polka Dots - Or Do They? by Debbie Dadey and
    Marcia Thornton Jones, Scholastic.

Older Readers (10 to 13 years of age)

Car by Richard Sutton, Knopf.
Carey's Fire by Lee Wardlaw, Avon.
The Dead Man in Indian Creek by Mary Downing Hahn, Clarion.
Don't Rent My Room! by Judie Angell, Bantam.

The Face on the Milk Carton by Caroline B. Cooney, Bantam.
The Fastest Friend in the West by Vicki Grove, Putnam.
Ghost Brother by C.S. Adler, Clarion.
The Ghosts of War by Daniel Cohen, Putman.
Is It Them or Is It Me? by Susan Haven, Putnam.
Jobs for Kids by Carol Barkin and Elizabeth James, Lothrop.
Marrying Off Mom by Martha Tolles, Scholastic.
Moonkid and Liberty by Paul Kropp, Joy Street.
More Than Meets the Eye by Jeanne Betancourt, Bantam.
The Mouse Rap by Walter Dean Myers, HarperCollins.
The Place My Words Are Looking For: What Poets Say About and Through Their
      Work selected by Paul B. Janeczko, Bradbury.
Polly Panic by Mary Francis Shura, Putnam.
The Random House of 1001 Wonders of Science by Brian Williams and
      Brenda Williams, Random House.
R-T, Margaret, and the Rats of NIMH by Jane Leslie Conley, HarperCollins.
Saving Lenny by Margaret Willey, Bantam.
Seeing Earth from Space by Patricia Lauber, Orchard.
Valentine Blues by Jeanne Betancourt, Bantam.
Weasel by Cynthia DeFelice, Macmillan.

Andrew and the paydid house
One day Andrew giet paet
and wiete to paet the house
he giet mise. wien he wes
dien. the house wes mise
to. but he like it. his
paris dient like it. but
Lest he Lrnd hiw to pate
sied Dad but Mom sied
not a vare god Jib but Andrew
sied but I like it. but
Lest I paet it. do you like
it.

──── **FIGURE 7-7** ────

Ryan's Story, "Andrew and the Painted House"

—— **FIGURE 7-7 CONTINUED** ——

STATUS-OF-THE-CLASS

Name	Monday	Tuesday	Wednesday	Thursday	Friday

D1= first draft; D2= second draft; A.B.= abandon; S.E.= self-editing; P.E.= peer editing; S.C.= self-conference; P.C.= peer conference; T.C.= teacher conference.

—— FIGURE 7-11 ——

Status-of-the-Class Record Form

WORK ACCOMPLISHED RECORD SHEET

Date	Work Planned for Today	Work Accomplished Today

WRITING SKILLS RECORD SHEET

Title of Piece and Date	Skills Used Correctly	Skills Taught

- **Picture interpretation**—use of familiar schema, e.g., "bedtime storytime schema"

- **Cartoon schema**—use of title, familiar cartoonist, familiar characters, expectation of humor

- **Letter-sound relationships** as you transform and use the new alphabet (e.g., ⌐ = *I*; ⊤ ⌐ = *t o*) or recognition of frequent letter symbol for sound, e.g., L = *e*, as in H*e*'s, asl*ee*p, com*e*s

- **Letter pattern–sound pattern relationship**—e.g., *s-ee* (consonant, vowel), *th-i-s* (consonant, vowel, consonant)

- **Rhyming ending**—familiar letter pattern, e.g., asl*eep*

- **Sentence context**—context clues from word sequence, e.g., "…how this *story* comes out"

- **Rapid recognition of word** after having completed part of word in sentence context—e.g., "I *just want* to see…"

WORD-ANALYSIS SKILL	K	1	2	GRADE LEVEL 3	4	5	6
Print Awareness							
Print Organization	***	**	*				
Page Organization	***	**	*				
Book Organization	***	**	*				
Letter Names	***	**	*				
Letter Recognition	***	***	*				
Phonemic Awareness	***	***	**	*			
Phonemic Segmentation	***	***	**	*			
Letter-Sound Relationships							
Consonants	***	***	***	**	*	*	*
Vowels	***	***	***	**	*	*	*
Letter Patterns and Rhyme		***	***	**	*	*	*
Syllable Identification							
Compound Words		***	***	***	***	**	*
Prefixes, Suffixes, Roots			***	***	***	***	***
Consonant Groups and Digraphs			***	***	***	**	*
Context Clues	***	***	***	***	***	***	***
Rapid-Recognition Vocabulary		***	***	***	***	**	**
Skill Application Through Wide Reading		***	***	***	***	***	***

Key: *** Major Emphasis—high probability of learning and development
  ** Minor Emphasis—continued development
  * Maintenance—reinforcement through wide reading

—— **TABLE 8-1** ——

General Learning Order and Placement of Word Analysis Skills

Students need to:

1. *Recall prior knowledge and previous experience*—Identify what they know; raise questions about what they do not know; and predict what text will be about.

2. *Organize information while reading*—Predict what information will be found; conform/adjust predictions; and relate new information to prior knowledge.

3. *Organize information after reading*—Respond to text in some important way; identify major concepts and ideas; perceive relationships between concepts and ideas; perceive relationships with prior knowledge; and understand relative importance of ideas.

4. *Synthesize and articulate new learning*—Arrive at new understanding and insights; integrate new understands into prior knowledge base; find out how much was learned; and establish base for further learning.

5. *Learn vocabulary that labels important concepts, elements, and relationships*—Identify new words and terms; identify known words and terms in new contexts; use new words and terms in meaningful ways; and relate new vocabulary to prior knowledge base.

6. *Produce or create something new and apply new information*—Work through new ideas in writing; build, make, create something new, or perform.

—— **FIGURE 9-1** ————————————————————

What Students Need to Do When Learning from Text

Teachers need to:

1. *Determine students' prior knowledge and previous experience concerning the topic at hand*—Provide means for students to articulate their prior knowledge base; find out what students already know; and determine the magnitude of difference between what students know and what is to be learned.

2. *Provide means for students to organize information while reading*—Focus students' attention; engage students in the cycle of predicting/reading/adjusting predictions/reading some more; and develop linkages between prior knowledge and new information.

3. *Provide means for students to organize information while reading*—Establish various means for students to respond to text; engage students in elaborative discussion and follow-up activities; and encourage and teach various organizational structures for recording information.

4. *Provide means for students to synthesize and articulate new learning*—Allow opportunity for students to talk and write about what they have learned; further develop linkages between prior knowledge and new information; and identify linkages between new information and what is yet to come.

5. *Identify and teach vocabulary that labels important concepts, elements, and relationships*—Allow students to identify words and terms they need to know; find out what words and terms students already know; develop linkages between new words and terms and prior knowledge base; and develop activities for students to use new words and terms in meaningful ways.

6. *Provide opportunity for students to produce or create something new*—Promote elaborative projects and activities; find out what students learned; and evaluate degree of teaching/learning success.

—— **FIGURE 9-2** ——

What Teachers Need to Do to Guide Students' Learning from Text

K	**W**	**L**
(Know)	(Want to Know)	(Learned)

STUDENT NAME _____ **GRADE** ___ **DATE** _____

OBSERVATION AND EVALUATION OF:

LISTENING   READING

(circle one)

Instructions: Circle the appropriate letter to describe how each statement fits this student during your most recent period(s) of observation.

U=Usually   O=Occasionally   R=Rarely

GUIDES SELF THROUGH TEXT
1. Makes predictions.   U O R
2. Supports predictions with logical explanations.   U O R
3. Uses both prior knowledge and text information to support predictions.   U O R
4. Changes and refines predictions as reading/discussion proceeds.   U O R

KNOWS HOW TEXT WORKS
5. Demonstrates knowledge of common text elements and patterns.   U O R
6. Draws inferences from spoken and written text.   U O R
7. Understands how to use various source materials and events
   appropriate to age/grade level.   U O R
8. Demonstrates fluency and confidence when engaged with text.   U O R

UNDERSTANDS SOCIAL ASPECTS OF MEANING CONSTRUCTION
9. Is aware and tolerant of others' interpretation of spoken
   language and written text.   U O R
10. Supports and maintains own position in face of opposition.   U O R
11. Participates in interactions to negotiate meaning construction.   U O R

USES RANGE OF STRATEGIES WHILE LISTENING/READING
12. Raises questions about unknown information.   U O R
13. Uses illustrations and/or other graphic information
    to construct meaning.   U O R
14. Relocates and uses specific information to support
    predictions, inferences, and conclusions.   U O R
15. Revises meaning as new information is revealed.   U O R
16. Uses a functional system to gain meaning for unknown
    words (e.g., context-structure-sound-reference).   U O R

This developmental inventory may be reproduced for classroom use.

—— FIGURE 11-2 ——————————————

Developmental Inventory—Listening/Reading. (Reproduced with permission from Ruddell, 1993, p. 212.)

STUDENT NAME _____ **GRADE** ___ **DATE** _____

OBSERVATION AND EVALUATION OF:

SPEAKING   WRITING

(circle one)

Instructions: Circle the appropriate letter to describe how each statement fits this student during your most recent period(s) of observation.

U=Usually   O=Occasionally   R=Rarely

GUIDES AUDIENCE THROUGH TEXT

1. Uses language markers to identify the beginning, middle, and end of spoken or written accounts.   U O R
2. Develops and elaborates ideas.   U O R
3. Uses descriptive names for objects and events.   U O R
4. Provides adequate information for audience understanding of events, ideas, arguments, and accounts.   U O R

KNOWS HOW TEXT WORKS

5. Demonstrates knowledge of common text elements and patterns.   U O R
6. Relates information in a logical sequence.   U O R
7. Uses language and sentence structures appropriate to text type and age/grade level.   U O R
8. Demonstrates fluency and confidence while speaking and writing.   U O R

UNDERSTANDS SOCIAL ASPECTS OF MEANING CONSTRUCTION

9. Understands and appreciates various speech and writing styles.   U O R
10. Adjusts language to clarify ideas (spontaneously or over time).   U O R
11. Participates in interactions to negotiate meaning construction and develop elements of text and style.   U O R

USES RANGE OF STRATEGIES WHILE SPEAKING/WRITING

12. Uses ideas and language effectively to show sequence of events, cause-effect relationships, and to support main ideas.   U O R
13. Revises extemporaneous speech or first-draft writing to arrive at a more polished product.   U O R
14. Develops cohesion through idea organization and language use.   U O R
15. Explores topics with some degree of breadth and depth.   U O R
16. Develops graphic, spoken, and written text that illuminates meaning.   U O R

This developmental inventory may be reproduced for classroom use.

—— FIGURE 11-3 ————————————————

Developmental Inventory—Speaking/Writing. (Reproduced with permission from Ruddell, 1993, p. 212.)

NAME _____ **AGE** _____

GRADE_____ **DATE**_____

1. What do you like to do at school when you can do anything you want to?
_____
_____

2. Do you like to read? _____ If you do, what are your favorite books?
_____
_____

3. Do you have any books of your own? _____ If you do, what is your favorite? _____

4. What do you like most about reading?_____
_____

5. How do you know if someone is a good reader?
_____

6. Check the activities that you like best.
a) Reading books _____
b) Listening to stories _____
c) Going to the library _____
d) Watching TV _____
e) Going to the movies _____
f) Going to the zoo _____
g) Playing outside _____
h) Playing with my friends _____
i) Playing with my brother or sister _____
j) Helping my mother or father at home _____

7. What do you like to do when you go home from school? _____
_____

8. Of all your toys and other things at home, what do you like best?
_____
_____

Why?_____

9. What are your special interests outside of school?_____
_____

10. If you could have three wishes what would they be?
a) _____
b) _____
c) _____

This inventory may be reproduced for classroom use.

—— **FIGURE 11-4** ——————————————

In- and Out-of-School Interest Inventory

1. **Omission of a word, part of a word, or punctuation as reflected in oral reading intonation.** Circle the word, word ending, or punctuation. Omissions may or may not be significant, depending on whether they interfere with meaning. Omission of word endings may be dialect-related. Frequent omissions will usually interfere with meaning.

    Example: She ⟨had⟩ wanted to take...
    ...and they mov⟨ed⟩ like water.

2. **Substitution of a word.** Draw a light line through the word and write the substituted word above it. This miscue is significant if it interferes with meaning.

    Example: Angela ~~was~~ ^{is} seven...
    Example: The women all ~~were~~ ^{wore} beautiful white...

3. **Insertion of a word, word ending, or words.** Place a caret (^) at the point of insertion and write the inserted word, word ending, or words above the line. This miscue frequently occurs as a child relies on his or her normal oral language pattern and expectations regarding the text. This is not significant unless the meaning is significantly changed.

    Example: ... to take ^{some} dancing lessons ...

4. **Teacher provides word, after five-second pause, or when you recognize that teacher assistance is needed.** Place a T (for *Teacher*) over the word supplied. This miscue is usually significant; frequent need for the teacher to pronounce words suggests the reading material is too difficult and/or the need to develop background knowledge and word analysis skills.

    Example: The women all wore beautiful ^{T} white...

5. **Self-correction of miscue.** Record the initial miscue as it is made. After the self-correction, circle the word and place a C above the circle. This miscue indicates that the child is actively monitoring the meaning construction process and applying "fix up" strategies to derive meaning.

    Example:...saw some dancers ⟨on in⟩^{C} TV.

6. **Repetition of a word.** Underline the word or words repeated using a reverse arrow. Word repetition is often a means children use to mark time in order to apply word analysis skills to the next word or group of words. This may indicate the need for reading material that is at a lower level of difficulty.

    Example: Angela was seven years old.
    ←...to take dancing lessons...
    ←

7. **Word-by-word reading and hesitation between words.** Place a check mark between the words or where hesitation occurs. Hesitation suggests a fluency problem, especially if the words are those that occur with high frequency. This may indicate the need to encourage practice with high-interest material at a lower level of difficulty.

    Example: Angela ✓ is ✓ seven ✓ years ✓ old.

Angela

Angela was seven years old.

She had wanted to take dancing lessons ever since she saw

some dancers on TV.

The women all wore beautiful white dresses, and they moved

like water.

Angela wanted to dance just like them.

The Text for Your Transcript:

Angela was seven years old.

She had wanted to take dancing lessons ever since she saw some dancers on TV.

The women all wore beautiful white dresses, and they moved like water.

Angela wanted to dance just like them.

Now, check your notations with our analysis below.

Angela ✓ ~~was~~ *is* ✓ seven ✓ years ✓ old.
←——————

She (had) wanted to take *some* ^ dancing lessons (ever) since she saw some dancers (~~on~~ *in*) TV.
                          C

The women all (~~were~~ *wore*) ✓ beautiful ✓ white ✓ dresses, and
                C   T
they mov(ed) like water.

Angela *wants* ~~wanted~~ to dance just like them.

A Trip to the Store

Bill and Jimmy were on their way to the store.

They walked down the street.

Jimmy said, "That dog is looking out the window."

"Yes," said Bill. "He is the worst one in town. I am glad
      he is inside today."

The boys came to the store. They went to the IN door.

Swoosh!

The door opened all by itself!

"Wow," said Jimmy. "Look at that! A magic door!"

"You are silly!" said Bill. "The new doors work by
      electricity."

"What's electricity?" asked Jimmy.

"I'll tell you later," said Bill. "Come on let's get the
      bread."

The boys' mother needed bread for sandwiches.

Bill looked for a long time. The bread had been moved to a
      new place in the store.

Then he spotted it.

But where was Jimmy?

A Trip to the Store

Bill*ly* and Jimmy were on their way to the store.

They walked down the street.

Jimmy said, "That dog is (looking) out the ~~window.~~ [won/wah/something] [guh/girl/mething]

"Yes," ~~said Bill~~ [Billy said]. "He is the (worst) one in town. I am ~~glad~~

he is ~~inside~~ [something] today."

The boys came to the store. They went ~~to the~~ IN door.

(Swoosh!) [sho]

The door opened all by itself!

"Wow," said Jimmy. "Look at that! A magic [T] door!"

"You are silly!" said Bill. "~~The~~ [That] new door(s) work by

electric(ity)"

"What"s electric(ity)?" asked Jimmy.

"(I)ll tell you later," said Bill. "Come let's*ly* *go* get the

bread."

The boy's mother needed bread for sandwiches.

Bill looked for a long time. The bread had been moved to a

new place in the store.

Then he ~~spotted~~ [stopped] it.

But (where) [thuh/wr] was [is] Jimmy?

───── **FIGURE 11-6** ─────

Rebecca's Miscue Transcript

186

After reading the passage, the following questions were asked, with Rebecca's responses noted.

1. What did the boys' mother need from the store? (factual)

   <u>some bread</u>

2. What made the door work? (factual)

   <u>electric</u>

3. Why did Bill have trouble finding the bread? (factual)

   <u>cause it moved to a new place</u>

4. Why did Bill think the dog was the worst one in town? (interpretive)

   <u>cause he might bite everybody that comes next to him</u>

5. Do you think Bill was older or younger than Jimmy? (interpretive)

   <u>younger</u>

6. Why do you think so? (interpretive)

   <u>I just think he's younger</u>

7. Where would you have looked for Jimmy? (applicative)

   <u>Look all over the store and in the cereal toy place</u>

8. What would you do if you did not find him there? (applicative)

   <u>I'd call the police and tell them all about the thing that happened, and tell them what he looks like and describe him. Then I'd drive in the police car and point out if I see him.</u>

	1607–1840	1840–1910	1910–1960	1960–1990s
1. HISTORICAL EVENTS	Jamestown, Declaration of Independence, War of 1812	Gold Rush, Western expansion, Industrial Revolution, Railroads, Civil War, Population 70% rural, Electric lights, telephone, radio, Urban movement begins	World War I, Great Depression, World War II, Television, Korean war, Technology, Launch of Sputnik, Jet air travel, Large urban populations	Civil rights movement, Vietnam war, Free Speech-movement, Moon landing, Federal support for education, Computers, Gulf War, close of Cold War, Poverty and health care key concerns
2. KEY INFLUENCES	Religious views, Patriotic views, New country	Expanding nation, Technology grows, Rural society, Schools needed and "school districts" formed, German-Pestalozzian influence, developmental view of children, Scientific movement in education begins	World view expands, Research in education, Child-centered curriculum (Dewey), Literacy awareness— World War II induction testing, Technology and communication, Lay critics (Flesch & Trace), Publisher impact on schools, Urban center needs	School integration, Federal funding for special programs, Minority group equality and justice, Research-theory in education, Technology, New immigration movement

— **TABLE 12-1** —

Historical Perspective on Reading and Literacy Instruction

	1607–1840	1840–1910	1910–1960	1960–1990s
3. MATERIALS USED	Hornbook, Bible, New England Primer (speller, moral sayings, catechism), Webster's Blue Back Speller Content: religious and patriotic Classroom: benches, poor lighting and heating	McGuffey's Graded Readers, Materials become more available Illustrations are used more frequently Content: still moralistic but expands to include literary, history, and geography selections Classroom: desks are fastened to oil-treated floor, Beginning of grade levels based on age	Basal reading programs, Language programs, Teacher manuals developed to guide instruction Content: wide range reflects technology Classroom: rigid seating arrangement but becoming more flexible, Concern increased for better lighting and comfort	Basal reading programs, Children's literature, Whole language approach, Supplementary programs Content: great range of story content, incl. minority and var. gender roles Classroom: use of movable seating, high concern for lighting and comfort
4. INSTRUCT. EMPHASIS	Letter-name knowledge, Pronounce Oral reading, "Spell Downs," Memorization of Bible; Letter-sound relationships, Art of elocution important to democratic government	Phonics and syllable work in isolation and context, Oral reading, Recitation of memorized passages, Handwriting emphasis, little composition, Beginning of achievement test use	Word analysis and comprehension emphasized, "Usage" main language emphasis, Reading groups by ability, increased use of testing, Concern for individual student	Word analysis and comprehension based on story context, Oral and written language are integrated, Formal testing used, Informal evaluation for instructional planning is emphasized, Increased teacher options and choices
5. TEACHER PREP.	Able to read and write, Good moral character, Usually a male	One- and two-year normal schools, Women enter teaching in large numbers for first time	Four-year teacher colleges and universities, School-district in-service, Advanced specialist work encouraged	Five-year preparation programs, more in-service and advanced degree work available and encouraged

—— **TABLE 12-1 CONTINUED** ————————————————————

BLM 12-2 (text p. 610) An Instructional Continuum of Beliefs About Reading and Literacy Development

Continuum of Beliefs for Instructional Approaches

Bottom Up (Skills orientation)	Phonics Program	Basal Reader	Literature-Based	Whole Language	Top Down (Whole literacy orientation)

<<<<Teacher Decision–Making>>>>

FIGURE 12-6

An Instructional Continuum of Beliefs About Reading and Literacy Development

CRITERIA	RATING (1–.5–0)	CHARACTERISTICS
Age appropriate		Realistic presentation of concepts
Child control		Actors not reactors; children set pace; can escape
Clear instructions		Verbal instructions; simple and precise directions; picture choices
Expanding complexity		Low entry, high ceiling; learning sequence is clear; teaches powerful ideas
Independence		Adult supervision not needed after initial exposure
Process orientation		Process engages, product secondary; discovery learning, not skill drilling; intrinsic motivation
Real-world model		Simple, reliable model; concrete representations, objects function
Technical features		Colorful; uncluttered realistic graphics; animation; loads and runs quickly; corresponding sound effects or music; study disks
Trial and error		Children test alternative responses
Transformations		Objects and situations change; process highlighter

—— **TABLE 12-8** ————————————————

Developmental Scale for Rating Computer Software

Evaluator _____   Date _____
Name of Program _____
Title of Level(s) _____
Recommended Grade-Level Use _____
Specific Materials Examined: teacher manual_____ , student text_____ ,
workbook _____ , other material _____

Criteria	Rating				
	Poor				Outstanding
1. Informed philosophy (meaning-based?)	1	2	3	4	5
2. Research and theory base evident	1	2	3	4	5
3. Range of objectives (beginning literacy, comprehension, vocabulary, literature and reader response, word analysis, writing, reading and writing across content)	1	2	3	4	5
4. Instructional strategies and activities provide for range of needs and interests	1	2	3	4	5
5. Quality literature and informational selections; cultural and ethnic diversity; varied gender role models; other forms of diversity	1	2	3	4	5
6. Materials and activities hold high potential for developing learning motivation and interest	1	2	3	4	5
7. Teacher's guide—quality and ease of use	1	2	3	4	5
8. Recognition of importance of informal observations and ongoing evaluation	1	2	3	4	5
9. Adaptability of program relative to instructional philosophy	1	2	3	4	5
10. Belief that program can be be used effectively	1	2	3	4	5

Total ratings for program _____

Summary observations:

TABLE 12-9

Instructional Program Evaluation Checklist

UNDERLYING BELIEFS AND ASSUMPTIONS ABOUT LITERACY LEARNING: EARLY AND BEGINNING READERS AND WRITERS

Our current understanding of how children continue their development into fluent literacy during kindergarten includes the following beliefs and assumptions (these are synthesized from discussions in Chapters 2, 3, and 7):

1. Children learn the language of written text by hearing and seeing written text and by experimenting with written text themselves.

2. Children acquire and develop picture and print concepts, a sense of story structure, and theories about how written language works as they invent and reinvent oral and written text forms, test current language hypotheses, and successfully negotiate meanings in transactions with text.

3. Children's language and literacy learning are mediated by social interactions and transactions with peers and with literate others.

8:30 – 9:00	**Centers**—art, reading, writing, science, play, mathematics. Children choose center and stay in that center for full half-hour. Circle rug available for reading center children to use.
9:00 – 9:15	**Clean up/settle down**—necessary cleanup is done, children go to their home table as cleanup is completed.
9:15 – 9:35	**Circle**—attendance, morning song, daily helpers appointed, calendar, weather chart, sharing, story/poetry.
9:35 – 10:05	**Snack and recess.**
10:10 – 10:40	**Group projects**—dramatic play, construction blocks, puppet theater, literature discussion circles, writing workshop.
10:45 – 11:10	**Music and movement/art projects/seasonal projects**—alternate singing, instrumental music, dance, music interpretation, papier-mâché projects, murals, finger painting, holiday plays and projects.
11:10 – 11:25	**Clean up/settle down.**
11:25 – 11:35	**Circle**—Reflections on the day, story/poetry.
11:35	**Dismiss.**

TABLE 13-1

Organization of the Kindergarten Day: Half-Day

8:15 – 8:30	***Settle in***—put folders in cubbies, store snacks and lunches, go to home tables.
8:30 – 8:45	***Journal writing and special words***—children share special words to go into their word banks. Everyone writes in her/his journal.
8:45 – 9:15	***Circle***—calendar, weather, attendance, sharing, story/poetry.
9:15 – 10:00	***Language arts***—story dictation, literature circles, story illustration, journal writing.
10:00 – 10:15	***Morning snack and recess.***
10:15 – 11:00	***Math, science, and social studies projects***—six tables with manipulatives and experiments/projects. Children choose tables and stay in one center for the forty-five-minute time block.
11:00 – 11:30	***Music.*** (Music teacher three days a week.)
11:30 – 11:45	***Clean up/settle down.***
11:45 – 12:30	***Lunch and recess.***
12:30 – 1:30	***Quiet time***—free reading, writing, and art or nap; quiet sharing of books, writing or art with a partner.
1:30 – 2:00	***Physical education/Spanish/8th-grade buddies***—physical education, Monday and Wednesday; Spanish, Tuesday and Friday; 8th-grade buddies, Thursday. (Physical education and Spanish teachers)
2:00 – 2:30	***Free play***—dramatic play, construction blocks, puppet theater, play centers.
2:30—2:45	***Circle***—reflections on the day, story/poetry.

—— **TABLE 13-2** ——————————————————

Organization of the Kindergarten Day: Whole Day

UNDERLYING BELIEFS AND ASSUMPTIONS ABOUT LITERACY LEARNING: BASAL READING INSTRUCTION

The basal reader approach for developing children's literacy includes the following beliefs and assumptions (these are synthesized from Chapter 12):

1. Children's acquisition and development of fluent literacy is best accomplished by their progression through a systematic, predetermined sequence of skills that are taught in conjunction with carefully selected short narrative and expository texts.

2. Children acquire and develop fluent literacy as they become increasingly proficient in the areas of word analysis, vocabulary, comprehension, language knowledge, content area reading, and independent reading.

3. Materials for developing children's literacy need to be selected from literature of high quality and presented in an ordered sequence of difficulty to support children's growing literacy competence.

4. Lessons for fostering children's literacy development need to include the following elements: (a) development of background information and vocabulary knowledge, (b) guided silent reading, (c) comprehension development, (d) skill development and application, and (e) extension and skill practice.

5. Children acquire and develop fluent literacy best by learning in small groups that are organized according to proficiency and matched to reading materials of comparable difficulty.

8:20 – 8:40	**Morning warm-up**—attendance, current events, sharing, weather, story/poetry
8:45 – 9:10	**Spelling**—self-collected spelling words
9:15 – 10:30	**Language arts**—three basal reading groups
10:30 – 10:45	**Snack, recess.**
10:50 – 11:30	**Math.**
11:30 – 12:15	**Social studies.**
12:15 – 12:50	**Lunch, recess.**
12:50 – 1:10	**Story.**
1:10 – 1:45	**Science.**
1:45 – 2:15	**Physical education (M,W).** **Music (T).** **Art (Th).**
2:15 – 3:00	**Group projects** (M–Th)—children working on self-selected projects stemming from interests developed from science, math, social studies, music, physical education, and art. **Library** (F).
3:00 – 3:15	**Sustained silent reading or writing.**
3:15 – 3:30	**Reflect on day, story/poetry, dismiss.**

—— **TABLE 13-3** ————————————

Organization of the Classroom Day—Basal Reader Instruction

	Monday	Tuesday	Wednesday	Thursday	Friday
9:15 – 10:00	Grp. A	Grp. C	Grp. B	Grp. A	Grp. C
10:00 – 10:30	Grp. B	Grp. A	Grp. C	Grp. B	Journals

TABLE 13-4

Scheduling Basal Reading Groups—Week 1

	Monday	Tuesday	Wednesday	Thursday	Friday
Week 2 9:15 – 10:00	Grp. B	Grp. A	Grp. C	Grp. B	Grp. A
10:00 – 10:30	Grp. C	Grp. B	Grp. A	Grp. C	Journals
Week 3 9:15 – 10:00	Grp. C	Grp. B	Grp. A	Grp. C	Grp. B
10:00 – 10:30	Grp. A	Grp. C	Grp. B	Grp. A	Journals

TABLE 13-5

Scheduling Basal Reading Groups—Weeks 2 and 3

UNDERLYING BELIEFS AND ASSUMPTIONS ABOUT LITERACY LEARNING: LITERATURE-BASED INSTRUCTION

Literature-based instruction includes the following beliefs and assumptions (these are synthesized from our discussion in Chapter 12):

1. Children acquire and develop fluent literacy by reading and responding to complete literary works of high quality.

2. Children read and respond avidly to literature that interests them even when the difficulty of given literary works does not match their apparent ability level.

3. Children do not need to understand every word of any text in order to construct full, rich meaning for that text.

4. Children as active theory builders and hypothesis testers will acquire all the requisite language and literacy skills for competent reading and writing in the course of their progression through many works of literature that interest them.

5. In the event that specific skills are needed for children's literacy development, these skills should be taught in the context of that immediate need.

9:15 – 9:20 **Focus, discussion prompts**—teacher guides response group discussion by focusing attention ("Create a group map that shows the mood of your story") or with response prompts ("As a group, find a section of today's reading that everyone in the group really likes. Jot down some reasons why the group likes that section.").

9:20 – 9:50 **Reading response group discussion**—children follow focus or prompt as major topic of discussion.

9:50 – 10:15 **Whole-class sharing**—the essence of each group's discussion is shared with class.

10:15 – 10:30 **Journal writing**—children reflect and record responses to their reading and discussion.

TABLE 13-6

Organization of the Language Arts Period—Literature-Based Instruction

UNDERLYING BELIEFS AND ASSUMPTIONS ABOUT LITERACY LEARNING: WHOLE LANGUAGE APPROACH

The whole language approach includes the following beliefs and assumptions (synthesized from Chapter 12):

1. Children actively seek to extend their own language and literacy abilities as they interact with the physical and social environments.

2. Children's language and literacy development are socially mediated through ongoing interactions and transactions with other learners and proficient language and literacy models.

3. Children acquire and develop fluent literacy as they participate in and use literate behaviors in active, naturalistic learning events.

4. Children acquire and extend language and literacy abilities interactively with all other learning; language and literacy instruction must necessarily be integrated with all other instruction.

5. Children acquire and develop language, literacy, and learning skills as they participate in learning events that incorporate language and literacy abilities.

6. When specific language and literacy skills are needed for continuing development, these skills should be taught in the context of authentic learning events.

8:15 – 8:30	**Attendance, opening, poetry/song.**
8:30 – 8:35	**Status-of-the-groups roll call—Theme cycle units—**check with each group leader about plans for the day and what the group expects to accomplish.
8:35 – 9:30	**Theme cycle projects—**each group engaged in inquiry and research on the topic and issues selected regarding environment.
9:30 – 9:45	**Projects meeting–whole class—**groups discuss accomplishments of the day, assistance they need, and plans for tomorrow.
9:45 – 10:15	**Book clubs—**Small-group and partner gatherings to share good books. Special interest groups (e.g., comic book collectors, mystery buffs) encouraged.
10:15 – 10:30	**Snack, recess.**
10:30 – 10:45	**Writing workshop Mini-Lesson and Status-of-the-class roll call.**
10:45 – 11:30	**Writing time and conferences.**
11:30 – 11:50	**Sharing time and Author's Chair.**
11:50 – 12:30	**Lunch, recess.**
12:30 – 12:50	**Story time—Read to students.**
12:50 – 1:50	**M, T, Th, F – Activity Centers—**group problem solving—integrated math, science, social studies, art, language arts. Children work in two centers each day. **W – Library.**
1:50 – 2:15	**M, W – Music.** **T, Th, F – Physical education.**
2:15 – 2:45	**M, W – Recess 2:15–2:30; free activity 2:30–2:45.** **T, Th, F – Free activity—**children read, write in journals, share a book or some writing with a friend, do follow-up project work, listen to music, use art center.
2:45 – 3:10	**End-of-day reflections—**whole group, story/song.
3:10	**Dismiss.**

—— **TABLE 13-7** ————————————————————

Organization of the Classroom Day—Whole Language Approach

PROJECT WORK MANAGEMENT SHEET

GROUP: _____

MEMBERS: _____

_____

_____

_____

_____

Date	Work Planned	Work Accomplished

— FIGURE 13-5 ——————————————————

Project Work Management Sheet

TEACHER STYLE	CHARACTERISTICS				CHANGE PROCESS
	COMMUNICATION WITH STUDENTS AND TEACHER PEERS	PERCEPTION OF SELF IN RELATION TO PEERS	MANAGEMENT STYLE/ MOTIVATION	PROBLEM SOLUTION APPROACH	NEW IDEAS/ CHANGE POTENTIAL
1. Supportive-Productive	Open, two-way interaction, seeks clarification and resolution	Equal	Cooperatively determined action, praise/high motivation	Intellectually curious, confidence in self, open consultation, internal locus of control/positive, high expectations	High/ high
2. Supportive-Nonproductive	Partially open, defensive, self-deprecating, self-inadequate	Inferior	Assigned action, praise, admonition/moderate to low motivation	Little curiosity expressed, relies heavily on work and support from others, external locus of control/moderate/low expectations	Moderate/ low
3. Nonsupportive-Productive	Partially open, defensive of personal beliefs, little concern for ideas of others, verbally aggressive	Superior	Use of authority, admonition/moderate to low motivation	Little curiosity expressed, rejection of others' ideas and provocation of others, internal locus of control/moderate to negative, moderate expectations	Low/ low
4. Nonsupportive-Nonproductive	Closed, defensive, hostile, conflict	Inferior, rejected	Use of authority, reprimand/very low motivation	Little or no curiosity expressed, overwhelmed by problem, external locus of control, low expectations	Very low/ very low

—— TABLE 14-1 ——

Teacher Styles, Characteristics, and the Change Process
Source: Based on Ruddell & Sperling, 1988, Table 2, p. 324.

Name _____

My child ____(Fill in child's name)_____

Phone _____

I would like to help in _____'s classroom in the following ways:

1. Classroom learning, working directly with students
___ listening to children read
___ taking dictation of children's stories or poems
___ assisting children as they do assigned work
___ going on short school field-trip walks with children
___ going on day-long field trips

2. Assisting a small group or individual students with a special project such as:
___ arts or crafts
___ drama (plays, puppets)
___ creative writing
___ music
___ storytelling and children's literature
___ photography or film-making
___ special hobby _____
___ other_____

3. Assistance with large school projects
___ carnival, fiesta (or special event)
___ fund-raising
___ student council
___ school newspaper
___ other _____

4. Special school-wide tasks
___ library assistance
___ office assistance
___ make phone calls
___ other _____

I will be able to participate at school on the following days and times:
Day: M   T   W   Th   F   Any day
Time: Morning time _____   Afternoon time _____

I cannot participate in your classroom on a regular basis but would be available for special events. _____

_____
Signature

— **TABLE 14-2** ———————————————————

Parent Volunteer Checklist Information

206

	STRENGTHS	EMPHASIS DESIRED	REFLECTIVE NOTES
1. INFLUENTIAL TEACHER CHARACTERISTICS			
1) Personal characteristics (energy, caring, self-expectations)			
2) Learner potential (understand student needs, learning expectations)			
3) Attitude toward teaching (enthusiasm, intellectual excitement)			
4) Life adjustment (concern for academic and personal problems)			
5) Quality of instruction (make material personally relevant, strategy oriented, engage students in intellectual discovery)			
2. READING AND LITERACY AREAS			
1) Reading and literacy process			
2) Early reading and literacy development			
3) Reading comprehension			
4) Vocabulary development			
5) Literature and reader response			
6) Writing development			
7) Word analysis			
8) Content-area literacy			
9) Language and cultural diversity			
10) Evaluation reading and literacy development			
11) Instructional approaches			
12) Classroom organization			

— **TABLE 14-3** —

Self-Reflection and Introspection Teaching Checklist